COUNTDOWN TO
CHRISTMAS

COUNTDOWN TO
CHRISTMAS

ACKNOWLEDGEMENTS

This book has been a great deal of work for all the contributors who found time in their busy schedules to write their chapters and recipes. The task of creative co-ordination was left to Charlotte Winby, a producer on **This Morning** who goaded, cajoled and generally chased everyone for their copy. Thanks are also due to Elaine Collins, who negotiated the contracts and set the book in motion. **This Morning** is a team effort and producing this book has been no exception, so many thanks to Malcolm Goff for the studio photography, and Anne Stirk, the home economist, as well as to all the contributors themselves.

First published in 1995 by HarperCollins*Publishers*

This edition published by Limited Editions 1995

Text © 1995 Granada Television Ltd
Photographs © 1995 HarperCollins*Publishers* Ltd
Stills from THIS MORNING © 1995 Granada Television Ltd

A catalogue record for this book is available from the British Library.

0-583 32090-2

For This Morning:
Creative Co-ordinator: Charlotte Winby

For HarperCollins:
Editorial Director: Polly Powell
Project Editor: Carole McGlynn
Design Manager: Caroline Hill
Production: Bridget Scanlon

Designed and edited by SP Creative Design, Linden House, 147 Kings Road, Bury St Edmunds, Suffolk IP33 3DJ
Editor: Heather Thomas
Designers: Al Rockall and Rolando Ugolini

Photography:
Food photography: James Murphy
Home economist: Jane Stevenson
Gifts and creative crafts photography: Di Lewis
Exercise photography: Peter Barry (copyright © Arrow Books)
Photographs of Richard and Judy on front cover
and page 6: Brian Moody

Colour reproduction in Singapore by Colourscan
Printed and bound in Italy by Lego SpA

Contents

COUNTDOWN TO CHRISTMAS

INTRODUCTION

Christmas is a very special time for us, both on **This Morning** and at home as a family. On the programme we give inspirational advice on preparing for the festive season. Our team of **This Morning** experts are brilliant at guiding viewers through what can often be a taxing period. Their ideas are clever and practical, and even after the seven years that the programme has been on the air they are still dreaming up new recipes and gifts which you can make yourselves at home. We hope that this book will inspire you too. It is full of tried and tested recipes, decorative ideas and even a special post-Christmas diet from Rosemary Conley.

We really enjoy Christmas on **This Morning**; the atmosphere is full of festive fun as you will see in the next few pages. The big day, when it arrives, is never a disappointment. There is a certain tradition to the chaos of Christmas Day in our household, and with four children it is always loud, messy and, in every sense, a family day.

Enjoy using this book – and, of course, have a very happy, hassle-free Christmas yourself.

Judy Finnigan

Richard Madeley

What you see on the screen for **This Morning** is just the tip of an iceberg; behind the scenes there is a dedicated and hard-working team. With the Researchers, the Producer for the day comes up with programme ideas and together they craft the content of the show. Meanwhile, the studio team of sound, lighting, cameras, make-up, props and design work together to ensure that the technical machinery of **This Morning** runs smoothly. There is a glimpse of some of the crew in the photos bottom left and top right. Top left you see three of the team dressed up for the Christmas pantomime.

This Morning has been on the air for seven years and each year grows in popularity. Many of the family of experts have been contributing from the start, like Susan Brookes (top right) and Charles Metcalfe (bottom left). The family of *This Morning* experts work together with much friendly banter, and this means that the programme comes across as being relaxed and enjoyable, and there is always plenty of laughter.

This Morning informs as well as entertains. An important part of the show is food, with Brian Turner and Susan Brookes being our key cooks. Helping with all their preparation is Anne Stirk, who ensures that the food always looks wonderful and appetizing on screen. She is featured in the top right picture with Brian. Susan and Brian have a friendly rivalry and tease each other, but they love each other really (see picture bottom left). The show may sometimes seem fast and off the cuff, but, in fact, all the items are carefully planned, as shown top left where Richard, Judy and Brian Turner are going through the script.

PART ONE

GETTING READY

Many traditional Christmas dishes are made ahead of time, like the cake and pudding. In this chapter, Susan Brookes and Brian Turner show you how to get ready for the festive season. There are many delicious recipe ideas that you can make in advance and store or freeze until the big day, as well as useful tips and expert advice that will help save you time and make your Christmas more enjoyable.

PLAN AHEAD FOR CHRISTMAS

SUSAN BROOKES

It sounds strange, I know, but you can't start your advance planning for Christmas until you know how you want to end up. So before you embark on your festive preparations, you should ask yourself the following questions. How many people will you be catering for, and for which meals? Will you be having a party? Will you have guests and visitors over the holiday period?

Sitting down with a diary, pen and paper now will not only save you hassle and time, but it will also save you money, as you should be able to cut down on wasted food with a little forethought. Don't forget to take left-overs into account in your planning; you may well find that there's more than you thought to spend on presents.

Personally, I tend to work backwards from that moment of huge relief when you put the turkey, in all its glory, on to the loaded Christmas table, knowing that when your family have worked their way through that lot you won't be called upon to provide more food, apart from the odd turkey sandwich, until the following day.

Of course there will be a last-minute rush – what Christmas was ever without one? However, there is a lot you can do in advance to eliminate any Christmas Eve panics. Many of the dishes in this book can be made ahead and stored or frozen until needed. Look at the Top Ten Tips compiled from the survivors of many Christmases, which I recommend you take into account.

TOP TEN CHRISTMAS TIPS

1 Don't try to do too much. Be realistic about the tasks you set yourself. Do you really need to offer four courses, or three choices of pudding? A friend once told me that she always had trouble keeping everything warm and having it all ready to serve together. I wasn't surprised when I discovered she served four vegetables with the turkey as well as all the other trimmings.

2 Cooking a meal is followed inevitably by serving it, so before you invite hordes of people to join you, are you sure that you have sixteen chairs, sixteen sets of cutlery, plates, etc? If you still say that you love a crowd, then think about who you will borrow from.

3 Getting carried away on the special dishes may lead you to overlook the obvious – I know, I've done it! One Christmas not long after I got married, the house was stuffed with exotic goodies and rich foods, but when we came down for breakfast on Christmas morning there was no milk to make a cup of tea and no bread for toast because I'd used the last of both to make bread sauce the day before! With everyone at home, you will use more of these everyday foods than usual, so make sure that you keep some space in your kitchen cupboards, refrigerator or freezer for basic standbys.

4 The most common mistake that most people make is going over the top, especially regarding the size of the turkey. I once had to cut the legs off a monster that we had been given in order to fit it into the oven. A good rule of thumb is to allow 450g/1lb of oven-ready weight per person. This will still leave you enough turkey for some left-overs but will avoid the cries of "Oh, not turkey again!" when it has been hanging around for too long.

5 When you are asked if there is anything that people can do to help, be specific. For instance, I always ask my

mother-in-law to prepare the sprouts and give her a corner of the kitchen table where she can work. There's nothing more irritating than the sink being monopolized for long periods by grandpa rinsing out coffee cups when you need to use it. You could also ask someone to take charge of the pudding course. Remember the golden rule: the best leaders know how to delegate.

6 It may not be possible to please everyone, however hard you try. With the mix of generations, family and friends, there's got to be some give and take. If you are inviting people into your home, then although you must take their feelings into consideration, it is ultimately your decision as to what time the meal is served and what food is offered. For example, do you want your Christmas meal as a late lunch or an early evening dinner? In this book, we give you recipes to suit every occasion, but only you can decide on the master plan.

7 Give your guests some choice, as far as is practicable. Obviously, you would check if anyone was a vegetarian, but there could be other diets to cater for, and if you offer some alternatives, especially for a party, rather than a simple take-it-or-leave-it menu, you will enable your guests

to avoid whatever they dislike. It can be embarrassing if someone says "No fish for me, thank you", and all you have to offer as an alternative is a boiled egg.

8 Many of the traditional Christmas foods are actually designed to be made ahead. For instance, most puddings and cakes improve in flavour with keeping. Some of the most festive recipes can be sorted out well in advance and are all the better for doing so. Many of the mouthwatering preserves and pickles featured in this book have to be made at least one month before Christmas. They can also double up as useful emergency presents. Other recipes, such as pâtés, pies, tarts and frozen desserts, can be made ahead and frozen.

9 Try to mix old and new. In my experience, it's strange, but true, that it's young people who are often the most traditionalist, wanting the same foods at the same meals as they've always had. There's something to be said for this, and it certainly gives you a useful framework within which

to plan and cook. However, try to look out for a different twist to an old favourite; tickle the old folks' fancy with something fresh and different – at the very least, it will give them something to talk about!

10 Lastly, try to remember that you are supposed to enjoy Christmas, even if you are chief cook and bottle washer. Providing food at such a special time of feasting is like giving love, and the season of goodwill extends to you, too. So get everyone to join in and help out; don't shut yourself off in the kitchen. Enjoy yourself!

PLANNING AHEAD

Much of the joy of Christmas lies in the anticipation. The preparations should be enjoyable, and I still try to make my Christmas cake when one of my daughters is around, as they always remember the fun they had as little children helping to stir the mixture.

Mincemeat, preserves, the classic plum pudding and rich fruit cake must be made in advance and left to mature before eating. All these dishes evolve from the time when the harvest, with all its goodness, was gathered in and stored in readiness for the dark winter days, which are brightened by the great feast of Christmas.

Most seasonal cakes and puddings benefit from being made at least a month before Christmas. Many pickles, preserves and relishes will also improve in flavour if they are bottled in advance and stored for a few weeks in a cool, dark place before opening. Therefore advance planning and preparation are not only wise but a necessity.

Most stuffings can be prepared and frozen before cooking, which will save you time on Christmas Day. Even breadcrumbs for bread sauce can be made from left-over bread when you happen to have some in the preceding weeks – they freeze very well.

In addition, you can plan some of your meals and menus for the holiday period weeks ahead, and cook some useful freezer standbys, especially in case unexpected guests drop in and you need to stretch a meal. Soups, stews, bakes, casseroles, pies and many other savoury dishes and desserts will freeze successfully and will help to keep last-minute preparations to a minimum. This will give you more time to relax and enjoy Christmas with your family and friends. Even the brandy butter can be made a few days ahead and then kept in the refrigerator until the big day; both sugar and alcohol are good preservatives.

STORE CUPBOARD IDEAS

I have listed here some of the foods that I find useful to have in as standbys for unexpected guests. Obviously, you won't need everything on this list, but it may serve as a handy reminder.

1 Onions: these keep well in a cool, dry place and are an essential ingredient in so many savoury dishes.

2 Canned chopped tomatoes and a tube of tomato purée: these will keep indefinitely and can be used to make sauces for pasta and meat.

3 Long-grain rice and dried pasta: use these for creating quick meals, especially when using up left-overs. Cold turkey makes a very tasty risotto.

4 Jars or cans of olives: these can be added to salads or savoury dishes, or handed round with drinks.

5 Long-life cream or Greek yogurt: these will give a luxury finish to sauces or can be served with many desserts and puddings.

6 Frozen puff pastry: keep a packet in the freezer as it may come in very useful in the days after Christmas. Use in sweet and savoury dishes, or for making party vol-au-vents.

A COOK'S ADVENT

You don't have to do all these things in advance, but you can try! You may even find that you enjoy all the preparations and Christmas itself all the more if you make the time and effort to get ahead in the weeks leading up to the festive season.

NOVEMBER

- Make the Christmas cake, Christmas pudding and mincemeat
- Clear some freezer space
- Check your equipment and recipes
- Make the preserves

EARLY DECEMBER

- Plan your festive menus
- Make any dishes that can be frozen

MID-DECEMBER

- Make the mince pies
- Marzipan and ice the Christmas cake

THE WEEK BEFORE CHRISTMAS

- Finalize your holiday menus and write your last-minute shopping lists
- Make more recipes that will freeze
- Clear out the refrigerator to make space

7 Parmesan cheese: buy this either in a block or ready-grated in a drum. It will keep for a long time in the refrigerator and is useful for sprinkling over pasta and other savoury dishes, as well as adding to sauces.

8 Herbs and spices: these can be used to flavour a wide range of savoury and sweet dishes, and add a new dimension to left-overs.

CHRISTMAS PUDDING

BRIAN TURNER

Every chef has a tried and tested Christmas pud, and here's mine. It's luxurious, rich and I love it. You may be surprised to find carrot in the list of ingredients but it helps to keep the pudding moist. What's great about this recipe is that you can cook it well ahead of time. In fact, you could make triple the quantity and then keep the spare puddings for the next three years! They don't spoil – the flavour just improves.

115g/4oz breadcrumbs
115g/4oz caster sugar
¹/₂ teaspoon ground cinnamon
¹/₂ teaspoon mixed spices
¹/₂ teaspoon ground nutmeg
225g/8oz candied peel, chopped
225g/8oz dried apricots, chopped
115g/4oz grated carrot
115g/4oz grated apple
grated rind and juice of 1 orange
115g/4oz shredded suet
225g/8oz raisins
225g/8oz sultanas
2 eggs
150ml/¹/₄ pint dry cider
1 tablespoon golden syrup

1 Put the breadcrumbs, sugar, cinnamon, mixed spices and nutmeg in a large mixing bowl, and mix well together. Mix in the candied peel and dried apricots, and then add the grated carrot and apple. Stir in the orange rind and juice, and the shredded suet, raisins and sultanas.

2 In another bowl, beat the eggs and mix in the cider. Warm the syrup and stir into the beaten egg mixture. Pour into the pudding mixture and stir well. Cover the bowl and leave overnight in a cool place to mature.

3 Grease a 1.5 litre/2¹/₂-pint pudding basin and spoon in the pudding mixture. Press down firmly.

4 Cut out a circle of greaseproof paper larger than the basin and use to cover the pudding. Tie it securely in place with string and then cover with foil to make the pudding watertight. Tie with string.

5 Place the basin in a large saucepan with enough water to come halfway up the sides. Steam the pudding gently for 6-8 hours, topping up the water regularly to prevent it drying up. Store the pudding, still covered, in a cool, dry place until Christmas.

Note: For reheating instructions on Christmas Day, turn to page 110.

SERVES: 8

A Healthy Christmas Pudding

Susan Brookes

This is the nearest I can get to a healthy Christmas pudding – no added sugar and the only fat is in the egg yolks. It is suitable for vegetarians and anybody on a wheat-free diet, as it is made without flour. The pudding will be moister and fruitier if you steam it, but it can also be cooked in the microwave.

350g/12oz sultanas
225g/8oz dried apricots, soaked and drained
1 x 420g/14oz can of prunes, drained and stoned
grated rind and juice of 1 lemon
115g/4oz ground almonds
115g/4oz pecans or walnuts, chopped
2 level teaspoons ground mixed spice
4 tablespoons brandy
2 egg yolks

1 Put 175g/6oz of the sultanas and all the apricots into the bowl of a food processor. Add the prunes and process until the mixture is well-chopped and roughly blended. Tip into a mixing bowl and add all the remaining ingredients. Mix well with a fork.
2 Line 8 small basins or 1 large 1 litre/2-pint basin with some baking parchment, and then fill with the pudding mixture. Smooth over the top, leaving a little room for the pudding(s) to rise. Cover each one with a circle of baking parchment. If you are going to steam the pudding(s), cover loosely with foil and secure with string; for microwaved pudding(s), use a larger circle of baking parchment and pierce it to let the steam escape. Tie in place with string.
3 To steam the pudding(s), place in a large saucepan with boiling water to come two-thirds of the way up the sides of the basin(s) or set in the top of a steamer over simmering water. Simmer small puddings for 1½ hours; 3 hours for a large one. Alternatively, microwave the pudding(s). A large pudding will take 10 minutes on HIGH in a 700-watt oven with 5 minutes' standing time; smaller puddings will take 5 minutes on HIGH. Serve the pudding(s) hot with brandy butter.
SERVES: 8

The Ten-Minute Christmas Pudding

Susan Brookes

Here's a useful recipe when you are in a last-minute panic. Make it on Christmas Eve, leave to stand overnight and cook the following day in ten minutes in the microwave.

75g/3oz plain flour
pinch of salt
pinch of ground cinnamon
pinch of ground nutmeg
1 teaspoon mixed spice
25g/1oz wholemeal breadcrumbs
75g/3oz shredded suet
75g/3oz soft dark brown sugar
50g/2oz chopped mixed peel
50g/2oz glacé cherries, chopped
50g/2oz currants
115g/4oz sultanas
150g/5oz raisins
50g/2oz cooking apple, peeled, cored and chopped
50g/2oz blanched almonds, chopped
grated rind and juice of ½ lemon
grated rind and juice of 1 small orange
2 tablespoons brandy
2 eggs, size 3
2 tablespoons black treacle
2 tablespoons milk

1 Sift the flour, salt and spices into a large mixing bowl. Add the breadcrumbs, suet, sugar, mixed peel, cherries, dried fruit, apple and almonds, and stir well. Beat in the remaining ingredients to form a soft dropping consistency. Cover the bowl and refrigerate overnight.
2 The following day, remove from the refrigerator and stir well. Pour into a greased 1 litre/2-pint pudding basin, and cover with cling film or greased greaseproof paper.
3 Place in the microwave oven and cook on HIGH for 10 minutes. Leave to stand for 10 minutes before turning out the pudding on to a serving dish. Serve with brandy butter.
SERVES: 6

TRIPLE CHOC SLICE

SUSAN BROOKES

This attractive dessert can be made several days in advance and then frozen until required. Chocaholics will love it, and it makes a wickedly delicious alternative to Christmas pudding.

450ml/15 fl oz full cream milk
6 egg yolks
175g/6oz caster sugar
few drops of vanilla essence
115g/4oz plain chocolate chips
115g/4oz milk chocolate chips
115g/4oz white chocolate chips
450ml/15 fl oz double cream
chocolate leaves, to decorate

1 Put the milk in a saucepan and slowly bring to boiling point. In a bowl, whisk together the egg yolks and sugar until pale and creamy. Add the vanilla essence and then pour the milk into the yolk mixture, a little at a time, whisking gently. Return to the saucepan and heat slowly, stirring continuously until the mixture coats the back of a wooden spoon. Take care that it does not boil.
2 Divide the sauce between 3 bowls, and allow to cool for a few minutes. Add the plain chocolate chips to one bowl, the milk chocolate to the second bowl, and the white chocolate to the third bowl. Stir the mixture in each bowl well.
3 Whip the cream lightly until it just starts to hold its shape, and then add one-third to each bowl of chocolate sauce. Stir well until thoroughly mixed.
4 Line an oblong freezer container with cling film and pour in the plain chocolate mixture. Freeze until solid and then remove from the freezer and cover with the white chocolate mixture. Replace in the freezer until frozen solid. Cover with the milk chocolate layer and freeze until solid.
5 To serve, remove from the freezer and cut into slices. Decorate with chocolate leaves. This delicious dessert can be frozen for up to 1 month.
SERVES: 8

Opposite: Triple Choc Slice

CHOCOLATE PECAN TARTS

BRIAN TURNER

300g/10oz sweet pastry
3 eggs
1 teaspoon vanilla essence
225ml/8 fl oz golden syrup
225g/8oz caster sugar
225g/8oz pecan nuts
50g/2oz melted butter
115g/4oz melted chocolate
icing sugar for dusting

1 Roll out the pastry on a lightly floured surface, and use to line six 10cm/4-inch loose-bottomed tartlet tins. If you don't have individual tins, you could use a 25cm/10-inch tart tin instead. Bake the tart(s) 'blind' in a preheated oven at 200°C/400°F/Gas Mark 6 for 10 minutes.
2 Prepare the filling: mix the eggs, vanilla essence, golden syrup and caster sugar. Add the pecan nuts, melted butter and chocolate. Mix well and pour into the pastry cases.
3 Place in the preheated oven, and after 10 minutes reduce the oven temperature to 160°C/325°F/Gas Mark 3 and continue cooking for a further 30 minutes.
4 Let the tarts cool in the tins before turning out. Sprinkle half of the surface of each tart with icing sugar, using a piece of card to protect the other half of the tart. If wished, the tarts can be made in advance and frozen for up to 1 month.
SERVES: 6

CHOCOLATE TIPS

● If you are going to the trouble of making a luxury, chocolate-based pud, buy the best chocolate you can find – it's worth it. Look for brands with a high cocoa content: with over 50 per cent cocoa solids.
● When melting chocolate, gently does it. Melt it slowly in a heatproof bowl over water that is just simmering, stirring with a wooden spoon. Or use the microwave, putting the chocolate in for short bursts.

Traditional Christmas Cake

Susan Brookes

1kg/2lb mixed dried fruit and peel
175ml/6 fl oz brandy
4 large eggs, size 1
225g/8oz butter, softened
225g/8oz dark soft brown sugar
1 tablespoon black treacle
350g/12oz plain flour
1 heaped teaspoon ground cinnamon
1/2 teaspoon salt
115g/4oz ground almonds
225g/8oz glacé cherries, chopped

For the glaze and topping:
115g/4oz apricot jam
assorted glacé fruit and whole nuts

1 A few hours before baking, or the previous day, soak the dried fruit and peel in 8 tablespoons of the brandy.
2 Whisk the remaining brandy with the eggs in a small bowl. Cream the softened butter with the sugar and black treacle in a large mixing bowl. In another bowl, mix together the flour, cinnamon and salt.
3 Add a little of the flour mixture to the creamed butter and sugar, and then a little brandy mixture. Continue adding the mixtures alternately until both are used up. Mix in the ground almonds, cherries and soaked fruit.
4 Pour into a greased and lined 20cm/8-inch square cake tin and bake in a preheated oven at 160°C/325°F/Gas Mark 3 for 1½ hours. Reduce the oven temperature to 150°C/300°F/Gas Mark 2 and cook for a further 1½-2 hours. You can test whether the cake is cooked by inserting a skewer into the middle – it should come out clean.
5 Cool in the tin and then remove and wrap well in greaseproof paper or foil. Store in an airtight tin. For an extra-moist cake, prick the cake all over with a thin skewer or knitting needle, and pour a little brandy over the top before storing.
6 To finish the cake, the week before Christmas, warm the apricot jam in a small saucepan over low heat. Push though a sieve and then brush all over the top of the cake. Arrange the glacé fruit and nuts in rows over the top, securing them in place with the jam. Use the remaining jam to brush over the top of the fruit and nuts.
SERVES: 12

Christmas Cake

Brian Turner

115g/4oz butter
115g/4oz soft brown sugar
1/2 teaspoon vanilla essence
2 eggs
150g/5oz plain flour
25g/1oz self-raising flour
175g/6oz sultanas
115g/4oz glacé cherries
175g/6oz currants
50g/2oz mixed peel, chopped
50ml/2 fl oz rum
1½ teaspoons glycerine

1 Beat the butter and sugar together in a large bowl until light and creamy. Add the vanilla essence and slowly beat in the eggs, gradually so that the mixture does not curdle.
2 Sift the two flours together and then slowly beat into the cake mixture. Add the remaining ingredients and mix well. Spoon the mixture into a greased and lined loose-bottomed 15cm/6-inch round cake tin. Smooth down and flatten the top of the cake with a wet knife.
3 Bake in a preheated oven at 160°C/325°F/Gas Mark 3 for 2-2½ hours. Test whether the cake is cooked by inserting a skewer into the centre – it should come out clean. Allow to cool and then store in a cool, dry place until you are ready to decorate it. If wished, you can 'feed' it occasionally by pouring brandy or rum over the top. For ideas on icing and decorating the cake, turn to page 23.
SERVES: 8

Opposite: Traditional Christmas Cake

DECORATING THE CHRISTMAS CAKE

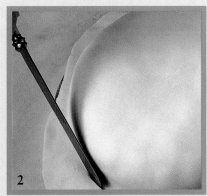

To ice the cake shown opposite, follow these simple instructions:

1 Brush the cake with warmed, sieved apricot jam or egg white and cover with almond paste (marzipan). Trim away the excess, cover with a clean cloth and leave for 2-3 days before icing. You can use ready-made almond paste, which is available from supermarkets.

2 You can cover the cake with royal icing or fondant icing (as shown here). The advantage of using fondant icing is that you can buy it ready-made. All you need do is just roll it out and cut it to fit. Brush the almond icing with egg white before covering with the fondant. Trim around the base.

3 Colour some leftover fondant icing green or dust some with gold, and cut into attractive leaf shapes with a novelty cutter.

4 Use the fondant 'leaves' to decorate the cake, fixing in place with a little paste made from icing sugar mixed with cold water.

ROYAL ICING

SUSAN BROOKES

This quantity of royal icing is sufficient to cover a 20cm/8-inch diameter round cake. You will need to make half as much again to cover a 25cm/10-inch square cake.

2 egg whites
2 teaspoons glycerine
750g/1lb 10oz icing sugar
1 tablespoon lemon juice

1 Put the egg whites and glycerine in a large bowl and beat with a fork until the egg whites look foamy.

2 Sift the icing sugar into another large bowl. Gradually beat half of the sifted icing sugar into the egg whites. Then beat in the lemon juice. Gradually beat in the remaining icing sugar, a little at a time and beating well between each addition, until the mixture is stiff and glossy and forms stiff peaks. A hand-held electric whisk will take the hard work out of this. Cover the bowl with a damp cloth and leave to stand for 1 hour. Use to cover the marzipan on the cake. You can either spread it evenly with a palette knife, or spike it up for a 'snowy' effect.

FRUITY LAYERED CAKE

SUSAN BROOKES

For a cake with a difference, try this unusual recipe. The coloured layers look very attractive when the cake is sliced.

225g/8oz glacé cherries
225g/8oz blanched almonds
grated rind of 1 orange
1 teaspoon ground cinnamon
350g/12oz mixed dried fruit
1 teaspoon ground nutmeg or mixed spice
225g/8oz glacé pineapple, chopped
50g/2oz chopped angelica
225g/8oz unsalted butter, softened
225g/8oz caster sugar
6 eggs, size 3
275g/10oz plain flour
5 tablespoons brandy

1 Put the cherries in a basin, and tip the almonds into another basin with the orange rind and cinnamon.
2 Mix the dried fruit in a third basin with the spice. Put the pineapple and angelica in a fourth basin.
3 In a large mixing bowl, cream the butter and sugar until light and fluffy. Beat in the eggs, one at a time, and then fold in the flour. Stir in 2 tablespoons of the brandy.
4 Divide the creamed mixture between the 4 basins and fold in well. Line a 20cm/8-inch square loose-bottomed cake tin (or a 23cm/9-inch round tin) with a double thickness of greaseproof paper. Spread a cherry layer in the base of the lined tin and smooth and level the top. Carefully pour the almond layer on top of the cherry layer, and smooth and level as before. Repeat with the mixed fruit layer, followed by the pineapple layer.
5 Bake in a preheated oven at 140°C/275°F/Gas Mark 1 for 1 hour and then reduce the oven temperature to 130°C/250°F/Gas Mark 1/2 for a further 3 hours, or until a skewer inserted into the centre of the cake comes out clean.
6 When cool, drizzle the remaining brandy over the top, and then store, well wrapped, in a cool, dry place. Decorate, if wished, with marzipan and icing.
SERVES: 12

LEBKUCHEN

SUSAN BROOKES

These delicious spicy ginger biscuit shapes are popular at Christmas time in Germany.

175g/6oz soft brown sugar
2 tablespoons orange juice
4 tablespoons golden syrup
2 tablespoons black treacle
2 tablespoons water
200g/7oz butter
2 teaspoons ground cinnamon
2 teaspoons ground ginger
575g/1¼lb plain flour
1 teaspoon bicarbonate of soda

1 Put the sugar, orange juice, syrup, treacle and water in a saucepan. Heat gently, stirring until the sugar has dissolved, and then bring up to the boil.
2 Remove from the heat immediately, and add the butter, cut into chunks. Stir until the butter has melted, and then add all the remaining ingredients. Beat well until you have a soft but runny dough.
3 Put the dough in the refrigerator to cool for at least 30 minutes. When cool, it should be firm enough to roll out on a well floured board. If it is too sticky, add a little more flour and knead well.
4 Roll the dough out 15mm/1/4-inch thick, and cut out shapes with pastry cutters. If you want to make the lebkuchen into Christmas tree decorations, cut a hole in each shape with a large straw.
5 Place the shapes on baking sheets lined with baking parchment, and bake in a preheated oven at 180°C/350°F/Gas Mark 4 for 10-15 minutes. Leave to cool.
6 You can glaze the biscuits with warmed apricot jam to make them shiny. Decorate with pieces of glacé fruit, sticking them in place with the apricot jam. Alternatively, you can pipe white icing around the shapes and decorate with silver balls. Store in an airtight tin for 2-3 weeks.
MAKES: 50 lebkuchen

Opposite: Chocolate Log

CHOCOLATE LOG

SUSAN BROOKES

175g/6oz plain chocolate, broken into pieces
6 eggs, separated
115g/4oz caster sugar

For the filling:
300ml/¹/₂ pint double cream
6 whole marrons glacés (candied chestnuts), chopped
1 tablespoon brandy or orange liqueur

For the topping:
300ml/¹/₂ pint double cream, whipped
2 tablespoons cocoa powder, sifted
50g/2oz dark plain chocolate

1 Make the roulade: break the chocolate into pieces and place in a basin over a pan of simmering water until it melts. Remove and cool a little.

2 Whisk the egg yolks until pale, and then beat in the sugar. Stir in the melted chocolate and beat until smooth. Whisk the egg whites in a clean bowl with a clean whisk, and then gently fold into the chocolate mixture.

3 Pour into a lightly oiled Swiss roll tin, which has been lined with baking parchment. Bake in a preheated oven at 180°C/350°F/Gas Mark 4 for 15-20 minutes. Do not overcook.

4 Remove from the oven and cover with a damp tea-towel. Set aside for 10 minutes. Invert the roulade on to a sheet of baking parchment and turn out. Remove the backing paper, and leave to cool. Trim the edges.

5 Meanwhile, make the filling. Whip the cream and stir in the marrons glacés and brandy or liqueur. Spread over the cool cake, leaving a border around the sides. Using the paper to help you, roll up the roulade like a Swiss roll. If wished, you can freeze the log at this stage in the paper wrapped in foil.

6 Make the topping: whip the cream and fold in the cocoa. Spread all over the roulade. Melt the chocolate and then drizzle it over the cream-covered cake to create a 'log' effect.
SERVES: 6-8

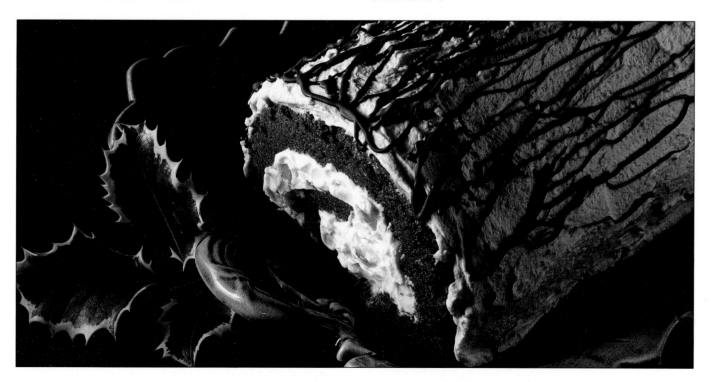

AMARETTO TRUFFLE TORTE

SUSAN BROOKES

I consider it a service to humanity to have adapted that fabulous chocolate recipe of Delia Smith's that everybody wanted to make if only they could find the liquid glucose! This gives equally luscious results but uses more readily available syrup. The addition of Amaretto liqueur complements the crushed Amaretti biscuits. You can make the torte in a round 23cm/9-inch cake tin but I find it handier to make two oblong puddings, each of which will serve four to six people, and to freeze one. Alternatively, it will keep in the refrigerator for three days.

450g/1lb plain chocolate
4 tablespoons golden syrup
5 tablespoons Amaretto liqueur
75g/3oz Amaretti biscuits
600ml/1 pint double cream
2 tablespoons cocoa powder

1 Break the chocolate into small pieces and place in a bowl with the syrup and Amaretto liqueur. Set the bowl over a pan of barely simmering water until the chocolate melts.
2 Meanwhile, crush the Amaretti biscuits finely. Line 2 loaf tins, 22.5 x 12.5cm/9 x 5 inches, with cling film, and

spread the crushed biscuits in the base of each tin.
3 Stir the chocolate, syrup and liqueur together until smooth. Allow to cool a little by pouring into another cool bowl and leaving for 5 minutes until it feels just warm and is smooth.
4 Whip the cream until it thickens and holds its shape, and then gently fold into the chocolate mixture until thoroughly mixed. Spoon this over the crumbs in the tins and leave in the refrigerator to set, either for several hours or overnight. You can freeze the puddings at this stage if wished.
5 To serve, turn the tortes out of the tins upside-down on to a serving dish. Sift one tablespoon of cocoa over each torte and then serve sliced with a little pouring cream.
SERVES: 8-12

CHRISTOLLEN

SUSAN BROOKES

This recipe comes from Austria, where Charles Metcalfe and I spent a memorable few days filming around Salzburg.

450g/1lb strong plain flour
pinch of salt
1 sachet 'easy blend' yeast
50g/2oz sugar
1/2 teaspoon ground nutmeg
225g/8oz sultanas
115g/4oz currants
50g/2oz citrus peel, chopped
50g/2oz blanched almonds, chopped
175g/6oz unsalted butter, softened
1 egg, beaten
grated rind of 1 lemon
4 tablespoons rum
250ml/9 fl oz milk, warmed to 'hand hot' temperature
175g/6oz marzipan

For the topping:
25g/1oz melted butter
50g/2oz icing sugar, sifted

1 Put the flour, salt and yeast in a large mixing bowl, and mix really well to distribute the yeast. Stir in the sugar,

nutmeg and all the dried fruit, citrus peel and almonds.

2 Add the butter, beaten egg, lemon rind and rum, and then add sufficient milk, a little at a time, to mix to a soft, but not too sticky, dough. Add a little more flour if necessary.

3 Knead the dough on a floured board for 10 minutes, and then roll out to a rectangle, approximately 25 x 20cm/10 x 8 inches. Roll the marzipan out to a smaller rectangle, 25 x 12.5cm/10 x 5 inches, and place on top of the stollen dough.

4 Fold one long side of the dough over the marzipan into the centre. Fold the other long side over into the centre, overlapping the bottom fold a little in the middle. Turn the loaf over, with the join underneath, and place on a greased

Above: Christollen

baking tray. Cover with lightly greased cling film and leave to rise in a warm place until doubled in size.

5 Remove the cling film and bake in a preheated oven at 200°C/400°F/Gas Mark 6 for 40 minutes, until well risen and golden brown. Cool on a wire rack and brush with melted butter. Dust with plenty of icing sugar and serve cut into slices. You can freeze the stollen if wished, or it will keep for 1 week stored in an airtight tin. If it goes a little dry, you can always toast it and serve hot, spread with butter.

SERVES: 10-12

MINCE PIES

SUSAN BROOKES

75g/3oz lard
225g/8oz self-raising flour
pinch of salt
25g/1oz hard margarine
350g/12oz mincemeat

1 Take the lard out of the refrigerator well before starting to make the pies so that it is not too hard. Put the flour and salt in a mixing bowl, and cut the margarine and lard into little pieces. Add to the flour and rub in with your fingertips. Add sufficient cold water to bind the pastry together, and then knead lightly.

2 Put half of the pastry on a lightly floured board and roll out thinly. Cut out 11 rounds with a 7.5cm/3-inch pastry cutter and use to line a greased bun tray.

3 Put a heaped teaspoonful of mincemeat into each pastry case. Use the left-over pastry and trimmings to make lids by cutting out rounds with a slightly smaller cutter. Cut 2 little nicks in each lid with a knife, and dampen the edges before securing in place. Press lightly round the edges of each pie to seal.

4 Roll out the remaining pastry and make 11 more pies in

the same way. Bake in a preheated oven at 180°C/350°F/Gas Mark 4 for about 15 minutes, until lightly coloured. Cool on a wire rack and then store in an airtight tin for up to 2 weeks. If wished, you can freeze the pies at this stage. To serve the pies, warm them in a low oven and hand round some cream or brandy butter.
MAKES: 22 pies

MINCEMEAT AND CHERRY TARTS

SUSAN BROOKES

115g/4oz unsalted butter, softened
225g/8oz plain flour
2 egg yolks
cold water to mix

For the filling:
400g/14oz mincemeat
2 egg whites (size 3)
115g/4oz caster sugar
50g/2oz mixed coloured glacé cherries, washed, dried and chopped
25g/1oz flaked almonds

1 Make the pastry: rub the butter into the flour and bind together with the egg yolks and cold water. Knead lightly until smooth, wrap in cling film and refrigerate for 30 minutes.
2 Roll out the pastry on a lightly floured surface and cut into rounds. Use to line greased bun tins and fill with the mincemeat. Freeze the pies at this stage, if wished.
3 Whisk the egg whites until stiff. Gradually whisk in half of the sugar and then fold in the rest. Fold in the glacé cherries, and pile the meringue on top of the pies. Sprinkle with the almonds and then bake in a preheated oven at 190°C/375°F/Gas Mark 5 for 20 minutes, or until the pastry is cooked and the meringue is lightly browned. The pies will keep in the refrigerator for up to 1 week.
MAKES: 24 pies

HOME-MADE MINCEMEAT

SUSAN BROOKES

450g/1lb crisp eating apples, e.g. Granny Smith's
grated rind and juice of 1 lemon
450g/1lb mixed dried fruit
115g/4oz candied peel, finely chopped
115g/4oz lexia raisins, chopped
115g/4oz dates, finely chopped
50g/2oz flaked almonds, chopped
1 teaspoon mixed spice
1 teaspoon grated nutmeg
4 tablespoons brandy

1 Peel, core and finely dice the apples. Mix in a large bowl with the lemon rind and juice. Add all the remaining ingredients and mix well.
2 Cover the bowl and leave to stand for 2-3 hours to allow the flavours to mingle and develop. Mix well and then spoon the mincemeat into clean, dry jars. Cover with wax disks and seal with airtight screwtop lids. Store in a cool, dry place for at least 1 month before using.
MAKES: 1kg/2lb mincemeat, sufficient to fill 24 mince pies

CRANBERRY AND MINCEMEAT STARS

1 Make up the pastry as for the Mincemeat and Cherry Tarts, adding 25g/1oz chopped walnuts to the dough and chill before using.
2 Mix the mincemeat with 115g/4oz fresh or frozen cranberries and spoon into the prepared pastry cases. Bake in the same way.
3 Roll out any remaining pastry and, using a small star cutter, cut out several stars. Brush with beaten egg, and bake on a lightly greased baking tray until golden. Stand the pastry stars on the cooked tarts, and serve warm or cold with whipped cream.

CHRISTMAS PUDDING ICE CREAM

SUSAN BROOKES

300g/10oz mixed dried fruit
115g/4oz no-soak dates, chopped
115g/4oz mixed glacé cherries, chopped
4 tablespoons brandy
2 teaspoons mixed spice
50g/2oz toasted hazelnuts, chopped
600ml/1 pint whipping cream
75g/3oz icing sugar, sifted

1 Soak the dried fruit, dates and cherries in the brandy with the mixed spice. Mix well together and set aside for at least 1 hour. Mix in the hazelnuts.
2 Whip the cream until it just holds its shape and fold in the icing sugar. Fold in the soaked fruit and stir gently.
3 Pour into a 1.5 litre/2¹/2-pint pudding basin, which has been lined with cling film, and freeze until firm. It can be kept in the freezer for 1 month.
4 To serve, turn the ice cream out on to a serving dish and leave in the refrigerator to soften for 1 hour before serving. Serve with Glacé Fruits in Rum (see below).
SERVES: 6-8

Opposite: Christmas Pudding Ice Cream

GLACÉ FRUITS IN RUM

Take a selection of glacé fruits, e.g. kiwi, mango, papaya, apricots, figs etc. Chop them roughly so that they remain chunky and place in a container. Cover with dark rum and leave to macerate for at least 1 week (up to 1 month if wished). Serve with the Christmas Pudding Ice Cream.

FIRE AND ICE

SUSAN BROOKES

As a child, I was always fascinated by the then-fashionable Baked Alaska pudding. How on earth did they get cold ice cream into the middle of a hot baked meringue? When I tried to make a Christmas dessert which would please not only the family traditionalists who wanted flaming brandy over rich, dark fruit, but also the people who yearned for something fruity or a refreshing ice cream, it all came together in this delicious pudding.

2 litres/3¹/4 pints soft-scoop vanilla ice cream
1 × 1.8kg/4lb rich fruit cake (20cm/8 inches square)
brandy for flaming

1 Keep the ice cream in the freezer while you line a 1.2 litre/2-pint pudding basin and 8 mini foil basins with cling film, leaving some overlap at the sides which can be folded over the top later.
2 Slice the fruit cake into long thin slices, about 1cm/¹/2-inch thick. Use these to line the sides and bases of all the basins. Don't worry if it crumbles – just push it together again and press it into shape to make a lining which has no holes and is no thicker than the original slices.
3 Remove the ice cream from the freezer and work quickly to fill the basins before it starts to melt. Press scoops of ice cream into each basin and press down with a spoon to fill any gaps. Fill each basin solidly almost up to the top.
4 Use the remaining slices of cake to cover the ice cream, making sure that it is completely enclosed. Wrap the edges of the cling film over the top and place in the freezer. Leave until firm and frozen, or freeze for up to 1 month.
5 Remove the puddings from the freezer 20 minutes before serving. Then turn them out, upside-down, onto a heatproof plate. Quickly warm some brandy (about 2 tablespoons per small pudding, or 150ml/¹/4 pint for a large pudding). Do not allow it to get too hot or it will burn off the alcohol and be more difficult to light. Set the brandy alight and pour it flaming over the puddings. Serve immediately.
SERVES: 16

HONEY-GLAZED HAM

SUSAN BROOKES

This delicious ham is a useful standby over the Christmas holidays. You can cook it a few days in advance if wished as it will keep in the refrigerator for one week.

2.2kg/5lb joint of ham, gammon or collar bacon
1 bay leaf
a few peppercorns
2 parsley stalks
2 onions, peeled
3 carrots, peeled

For the glaze:
50g/2oz soft dark brown sugar
5ml/1 teaspoon dry mustard
30ml/2 tablespoons clear honey

YORKSHIRE SAUCE

SUSAN BROOKES

2 oranges
175ml/6 fl oz port
pinch of ground cinnamon
75g/3oz redcurrant jelly
1 tablespoon brown sauce
salt and pepper

1 Peel the oranges and infuse the rind in the port for 1 hour. Squeeze the juice out of the oranges and set aside.
2 Pour the port into a small saucepan and add the remaining ingredients. Heat gently, stirring, over low heat until the redcurrant jelly has melted.
3 Serve with ham or pheasant. This sauce can be made in advance and stored in the refrigerator in an airtight jar for up to 3 weeks.
MAKES: 300ml/¹/2 pint sauce

1 Soak the ham overnight in cold water. The following day, drain the ham and place in a large saucepan. Cover with fresh water, and add the bay leaf, peppercorns, parsley, onions and carrots. Bring to the boil and simmer for 25 minutes per 450g/1lb, until tender.
2 Preheat the oven to 220°C/425°F/Gas Mark 7. Remove the ham from the saucepan and drain well, saving the stock for making soups. Remove the rind and score the remaining fat with a knife into a diamond pattern. Mix the glaze ingredients together and spread over the ham.
3 Place the ham in a roasting pan and cook in the preheated oven for 10-15 minutes, or until the glaze has caramelized. Serve hot with Yorkshire Sauce (see below) or cold with salad and chutney. To store the ham, wrap it in greaseproof paper or foil and keep in the refrigerator.
SERVES: 10

BOMBED BEEF

SUSAN BROOKES

The name of this recipe is derived from the traditional method of preserving a large piece of meat in a mixture of sea salt and salt petre. However, when I asked the chemist for salt petre, I got some very strange looks. Apparently, these days it is an ingredient used in making bombs! However, the recipe works perfectly well using just salt. It is best to start curing the meat ten days before you want to eat it, although it will keep fresh in a cool place for up to two weeks.

75g/3oz light brown sugar
2.25kg/5-6lb joint of beef, e.g. silverside or topside
25g/1oz black peppercorns
15g/¹/2 oz allspice
25g/1oz juniper berries
115g/4oz rock salt or sea salt

1 Rub the brown sugar over the surface of the beef to cover it completely. Cover and leave in a large stoneware crock or bowl in a cool larder or the refrigerator for 2 days.
2 Crush the peppercorns, allspice and juniper berries in a mortar with a pestle (or in an electric grinder) until powdery. Rub them into the surface of the meat with the salt. Leave,

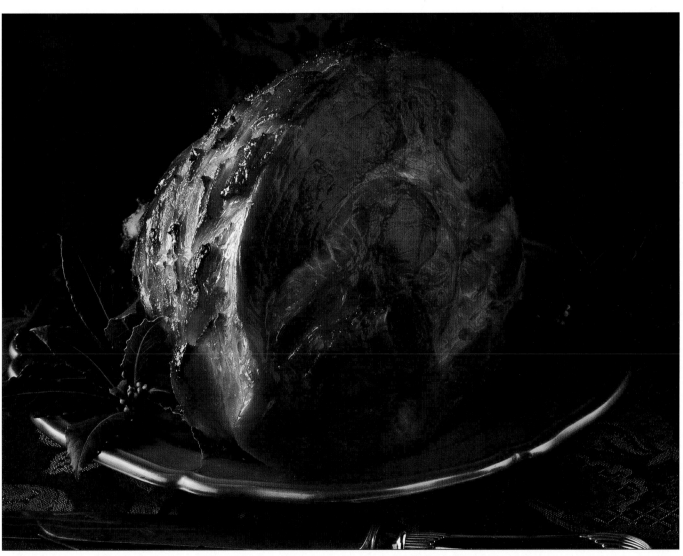

Above: Honey-glazed Ham

covered, in a cool place and turn the beef every day, rubbing the spices well into it, for the next 9 days. A liquid will run out of the meat and it will get darker in colour.

3 When ready to cook the beef, remove from the crock and brush off the spices. Wrap it in a double layer of foil so that it is well sealed and transfer to a large ovenproof pot. Pour 300ml/^{1}/$_2$ pint of water around it and cover with a lid. Cook in a preheated oven at 140°C/275°F/Gas Mark 1 for 4 hours. Remove from the oven and cool. Pour off the fat and liquid and press the beef between weighted boards. Serve cold the following day. You can store the beef in the refrigerator for 2 weeks.

SERVES: 10-12

Note: For a larger joint of beef, say 5-6kg/10-12lb, just double the quantities of sugar, salt and spices and cook for 6 hours at the same oven temperature.

STILTON AND WALNUT PIE

SUSAN BROOKES

For the pastry:
350g/12oz flour
175g/6oz butter, softened
1 egg (size 3), for glazing

For the filling:
1 small onion, finely chopped
2 tablespoons oil
2 eggs (size 3), beaten
350g/12oz cream cheese
1 small bunch of parsley, chopped
175g/6oz walnuts, chopped
175g/6oz Stilton cheese, rind removed and crumbled
salt and freshly ground black pepper

To garnish:
sticks of celery, watercress and sliced apples

1 Make the pastry: sift the flour into a bowl and rub in the butter. Add sufficient cold water to bind it and knead lightly. Cover the pastry and chill in the refrigerator while you make the filling.

2 Fry the onion in the oil until softened. Mix the eggs, cream cheese and parsley together, beating until smooth. Add the fried onion, walnuts and Stilton, and season to taste.

3 Grease a 23cm/9-inch round pie dish or deep loose-bottomed quiche tin. Roll out half of the pastry and use to line the base and sides.

4 Fill with the cheesey filling and smooth it level. Cover the pie with the remaining pastry, sealing the edges with a little water. Use the pastry trimmings to make leaf shapes for decoration. Brush the top of the pie with the beaten egg glaze and bake in a preheated oven at 190°C/375°F/Gas Mark 5 for 45 minutes.

5 Allow to cool in the tin. Serve the pie warm or cold garnished with celery, watercress and apple. If wished, you can freeze the cooked pie for up to 4 weeks. It is a splendid standby for vegetarian guests.
SERVES: 8

LEEK AND GRUYERE TART

BRIAN TURNER

This is an excellent tart to make ahead of time and, like the recipe opposite, a useful standby for vegetarians. It can be frozen for up to one month.

1 × 25cm/10-inch savoury pastry flan case
50g/2oz unsalted butter
4 leeks, well washed, trimmed and sliced
2 eggs
150ml/¹/₄ pint milk
150ml/¹/₄ pint double cream
salt and freshly ground black pepper
grated nutmeg
75g/3oz Gruyère cheese, grated

Above: Leek and Gruyère Tart

1 Fill the uncooked pastry case with paper and baking beans and bake 'blind' for 10 minutes in a preheated oven at 180°C/350°F/Gas Mark 4. Remove the beans and paper and leave the pastry case to cool and set.
2 Melt the butter in a saucepan and add the sliced leeks. Cover the pan and stew gently until soft, taking care that they do not brown. Remove from the heat and cool.
3 Whisk together the eggs, milk and cream. Add the seasoning and nutmeg. Stir in the cooked leeks and then adjust the seasoning to taste.
4 Pour the leek mixture into the flan case and sprinkle with the grated cheese. Bake in the preheated oven at 180°C/350°F/Gas Mark 4 for 35-45 minutes, until golden brown. Serve the tart warm or cold.
SERVES: 6-8

TUNA TERRINE NICOISE STYLE

BRIAN TURNER

This terrine is wholesome and chunky, and will bring many of the distinctive flavours of the Mediterranean to your Christmas table. Although it cannot be made weeks in advance it makes a delicious first course for dinner on Christmas Eve. You can make it two to three days ahead.

1 × 225g/8oz can of tuna in oil or brine
225g/8oz boiled new potatoes
2 red peppers
4 hard-boiled eggs, quartered
115g/4oz cooked thin green beans, chopped
1 shallot, chopped
12 green olives, stoned
150ml/¹/₄ pint mayonnaise
juice of ¹/₂ lemon
1 tablespoon chopped parsley
1 glass dry white wine
6 leaves, or 2 sachets of gelatine
salad leaves, to garnish

1 Line a 450g/1lb terrine tin, or loaf tin, with cling film. Drain the tuna and discard the oil or brine. Cut the potatoes into thick slices. Grill the red peppers until the skins are charred and blackened, turning them occasionally. Remove and cool in a polythene bag. Skin the peppers, removing the seeds and cores, and cut the flesh into thin strips.
2 Place the pepper strips in a bowl and mix with the tuna and potatoes. Add the boiled eggs, green beans, shallot, olives and mayonnaise. Stir in the lemon juice and parsley.
3 Put the white wine in a small saucepan, bring to the boil and then remove from the heat. Soften the gelatine in 2 tablespoons of cold water and then add to the wine.
4 Stir the gelatine mixture into the vegetables. Check the seasoning and then spoon into the prepared tin. Cover with cling film and leave to set in the refrigerator. Serve the terrine sliced with a garnish of salad leaves.
SERVES: 8-10

ANCHOVY NIBBLES

SUSAN BROOKES

2 × 50g/2oz cans of anchovy fillets, drained
4 tablespoons milk
350g/12oz packet puff pastry
2 tablespoons double cream
freshly ground black pepper
1 egg yolk, beaten

1 Cut the anchovies in half lengthways and soak them in the milk. Roll out the puff pastry 2mm/¹/₈-inch thick. Brush a 5cm/2-inch wide strip of the pastry with a little of the cream and lay some of the anchovy fillets along the strip near the edge. Grind some black pepper over the top and then cut off the creamed section. Roll up into a long sausage and seal the edge with a fork. Cut into 2.5cm/1-inch lengths and snip the tops with scissors. Repeat with the remaining pastry and anchovies until they are all used up.
2 Place on a greased baking sheet and leave to stand in a cool place for 1 hour. Bake in a preheated oven at 220°C/425°F/Gas Mark 7 for 10 minutes, until risen and golden brown. Cool before serving or freezing.

RICH MUSHROOM PÂTÉ

SUSAN BROOKES

a handful of dried porcini mushrooms (about 10g/¹/₂oz)
225g/8oz peeled onions
115g/4oz butter
900g/2lb mushrooms (preferably open caps)
1 litre/1²/₃ pints robust red wine
salt and freshly ground black pepper

1 Reconstitute the dried porcini according to the packet instructions. Usually, this is done by soaking them in warm milk and water for 30 minutes.
2 Chop the peeled onions finely in a food processor, with the metal blade fitted. Sweat them in the butter in a large

Above: Tuna Terrine Niçoise Style

saucepan for 10 minutes, stirring occasionally.
3 Chop the mushrooms finely in the food processor, and then add to the onions in the pan. Stir well and cook very gently over low heat. Drain the porcini and snip with scissors into small pieces. Add to the mushroom mixture in the pan with the red wine.
4 Leave to simmer over low heat, uncovered, for approximately 2 hours, stirring from time to time. The liquid should evaporate gradually until the mixture seems almost dry. Take care that it does not stick to the base of the pan and burn. Season to taste with salt and pepper.

5 Pot the pâté in a 1.8 litre/2-pint terrine dish or individual ramekin dishes, if preferred. Leave to cool and then cover and refrigerate; it will keep for up to 1 week in the refrigerator. Alternatively, freeze it until required; it can be frozen for up to 1 month. Serve very simply with toast or bread, or use it to stuff tomatoes and baked peppers. It is delicious served in a hollowed-out and toasted muffin or brioche, which you can brush with garlic oil before toasting.
SERVES: 8-10

PRESERVING

Home-made preserves, attractively bottled in pretty jars, make welcome gifts and are always appreciated. Follow these guidelines for successful preserving, and pickles, chutneys and preserves should come out of store even more delicious than when they went in as the flavours will have had time to develop and mature.

1 Always use sparkling clean jars. If possible, put them through the hot cycle in the dishwasher which will leave them really clean and warm, and ready for use. Alternatively, wash the jars thoroughly in clean, soapy water and then rinse and dry with a clean cloth. Place upright, but not touching, on a baking tray in a medium oven for 10 minutes. Fill the jars while they are still warm.

2 Recipes containing vinegar are slightly corrosive of metal, so don't put pickles and chutneys (nor the onion confiture) into jars with metal lids. Nor should you cover them with paper or cellophane jampot covers as the vinegar will evaporate eventually and the chutney will shrink. Cover the chutney or pickle with a waxed paper disc before screwing on the plastic lid.

3 Always store the jars in a cool, dark place which is free from damp. An old-fashioned larder is ideal, but if you don't have one, try to find a space in a cool room – perhaps under the bed in a spare bedroom!

4 Don't forget to wipe clean the outside of each jar when it has been filled and covered, in case of spillage. You should fill the jars right up to the top, leaving as little air space as possible.

5 Label the jars; you may know what they contain now but will other people? And will you remember in a month's time?

6 When making jams and conserves, you can test for setting point by putting a teaspoonful of the mixture on to a cool saucer and placing it in the refrigerator for 30 seconds. Push the surface with your finger; it should wrinkle if setting point has been reached.

APRICOT CHUTNEY

SUSAN BROOKES

450g/1lb no-soak dried apricots
juice of 2 limes
600ml/1 pint ready-spiced vinegar
225g/8oz soft brown sugar
2 cinnamon sticks

1 Chop the apricots roughly into halves or quarters and soak them in the lime juice for at least 30 minutes.
2 Heat the vinegar, sugar and cinnamon in a saucepan over gentle heat until the sugar dissolves, and then bring to the boil. Boil for 15 minutes, by which time the liquid should have thickened slightly.
3 Stir in the apricots and simmer for 15 minutes. Keep checking to make sure that it does not boil dry. Add a little more vinegar if the mixture gets too stiff.
4 Remove from the heat and allow to cool a little. Discard the cinnamon sticks, and pour the warm chutney into clean, warmed jars. Cover, label and store in a cool place for 3 weeks before eating.
MAKES: 3 × 450g/1lb jars

CONFITURE D'OIGNONS

SUSAN BROOKES

1kg/2lb onions
3 tablespoons olive oil
3 tablespoons vegetable oil
2 teaspoons salt
3 cloves
225g/8oz caster sugar
150ml/¹/₄ pint raspberry vinegar
200ml/¹/₃ pint red wine

1 Peel the onions and slice them thinly. Heat the oils gently in a large saucepan, and add the onions, salt and cloves. Stir well, cover the pan and leave to cook gently for 20 minutes, stirring occasionally.

with the metal blade fitted, or mince them coarsely.

2 Transfer to a saucepan with the cranberries and water, and bring to the boil. Reduce the heat and simmer gently for 15 minutes, or until the pieces of orange peel have softened. Remove from the heat and add the chopped nuts and sugar. Stir until the sugar dissolves.

3 Bring back to the boil and then boil rapidly for about 10 minutes, or until setting point is reached. Remove from the heat and cool a little before potting in clean, warm jars. Store for 2 weeks before eating.

MAKES: 3 × 450g/1lb jars

PEAR AND PEPPER CHUTNEY

SUSAN BROOKES

2kg/4lb pears, peeled, cored and chopped
450g/1lb onions, finely chopped
450g/1lb tomatoes, chopped
2 green peppers, seeded and chopped
450g/1lb demerara sugar
225g/8oz raisins
2 garlic cloves, crushed
pinch of cayenne pepper
1 tablespoon grated root ginger
900ml/ 1 1/2 pints ready-spiced pickling vinegar
15g/1/2oz salt

1 Put the pears, onions and tomatoes in an aluminium preserving pan or a large thick-bottomed saucepan. Cook very gently in their own juices for about 20 minutes, or until they are softened and reduced.

2 Add the remaining ingredients and continue cooking gently for about 1 1/2 hours, or until the chutney is thick, stirring occasionally. You can test whether it is ready by making a furrow in the surface with a wooden spoon; it should take just a moment to fill in.

3 Pour the chutney into warm, clean jars, cover and label. Store in a cool, dark place for at least 1 month, preferably 2 months, before eating with cheese or meat.

MAKES: 6 × 450g/1lb jars

2 Add the sugar, vinegar and wine, and cook gently, uncovered, for a further 40 minutes, stirring occasionally. The mixture will reduce and thicken slightly as it cooks.

3 When all the liquid has been absorbed or evaporated, remove from the heat and discard the cloves. When cool, pour into clean, warm jars and cover and seal. Store in a cool, dark place for at least a week and up to 2 months before serving with cold meats or cheese.

MAKES: 3-4 × 450g/1lb jars

CRANBERRY AND PECAN CONSERVE

SUSAN BROOKES

2 large oranges
450g/1lb cranberries
300ml/1/2 pint water
115g/4oz pecans or walnuts, chopped
350g/12oz sugar

1 Wash and dry the oranges, cut into quarters and discard any pips. Chop both the flesh and peel in a food processor,

PART TWO

GIFTS TO GIVE

There is great pleasure in giving and receiving gifts – even better when the gifts and cards are hand-made. In the following pages, you will find ideas for a wide range of edible and creative gifts with simple instructions on how to make them, whether it's a box of delicious home-made chocolates, a bottle of aromatic oil or herb vinegar, a scented pomander or a framed silhouette of your children.

CHOCOLATES AND SWEETS

QUICK AND EASY CHOCOLATES

SUSAN BROOKES

1 small decorated chocolate cake (from the supermarket),
15cm/6 inches in diameter
1 heaped tablespoon ground almonds
1 heaped tablespoon icing sugar
1 tablespoon orange juice
cocoa or chocolate vermicelli for coating

1 Break up the cake into crumbs with your fingers over a large bowl. Add the ground almonds, icing sugar and orange juice, and mix together to form a paste.
2 Take small spoonfuls of the mixture and roll into balls in your hands. Roll in cocoa or vermicelli, until evenly coated. Leave in the refrigerator until set.
MAKES: 20

CHOCOLATE TRUFFLES

SUSAN BROOKES

175g/6oz plain chocolate
110ml/4 fl oz double cream
1 teaspoon brandy, liqueur or orange juice
225g/8oz white or milk chocolate

1 Break the plain chocolate into pieces and place in a bowl over a pan of simmering water, until melted and smooth. Remove from the heat immediately.
2 Beat in the cream, a little at a time, and then stir in the brandy, liqueur or orange juice. Mix well and then place in the refrigerator for at least 30 minutes, or until firm. Take spoonfuls of the mixture and form into small balls. Alternatively, pour into small moulds to set. Chill.
3 Meanwhile, melt the remaining chocolate in a bowl over simmering water. Roll or dip the chilled balls in the melted chocolate. Chill until required. Eat within 3-4 days.
MAKES: 10-12

CHOCOLATE TORTE

BRIAN TURNER

In many European countries, it is traditional to take a dessert when you visit friends for lunch or dinner. If you don't want to make the full dessert, you can make the torte mixture, hand roll into balls and then roll them in cocoa powder when set to make mouthwatering truffles.

75ml/3 fl oz brandy
110ml/4 fl oz water
pinch of salt
110ml/4 fl oz glucose (or caster sugar)
115g/4oz plain chocolate
3 leaves of gelatine, or $^1/_2$ teaspoon, or $^1/_2$ sachet
110ml/4 fl oz double cream, whipped
1 × 25cm/10-inch round plain sponge cake
sugar syrup (made from equal quantities sugar and
water boiled together)
50g/2oz apricot jam

1 Put the brandy, water and salt in a saucepan with the glucose or caster sugar. Stir well over low heat until thoroughly mixed and then bring to the boil. Remove from the heat. Break the chocolate into small pieces and stir into the glucose mixture.
2 Soak the gelatine in a little hot water and then add to the hot chocolate liquid. Beat well until it cools. Mix in the whipped cream. Set aside until it starts to set.
3 Cut the sponge cake in half, place in a 25cm/10-inch round cake tin, trimming to fit, and sprinkle with sugar syrup. Spread with jam and use to sandwich the sponges together. Pour the chocolate mixture over the top and leave to set. Use a hot knife to cut the torte into slices.
SERVES: 10-12

CHOCOLATE TILES

SUSAN BROOKES

175g/6oz butter
200g/7oz plain chocolate
200g/7oz Rich Tea biscuits
115g/4oz mixed nuts, chopped
115g/4oz raisins

For the topping:
115g/4oz plain chocolate
25g/1oz butter
115g/4oz milk chocolate

1 To make the base, melt the butter and plain chocolate together in a bowl over a pan of barely simmering water.

2 Crush the biscuits into crumbs, and mix them into the melted butter and chocolate. Stir in the nuts and raisins, and then spoon into a foil lined baking tin, 28 x 20cm/11 x 8 inches. Press down well and smooth the top.
3 Make the topping: break the plain chocolate into a bowl with half of the butter and melt over a pan of simmering water. Repeat in another bowl with the milk chocolate and the remaining butter. Using a teaspoon, spread the two chocolates in alternate stripes over the crumb base. Create a feathered effect by dragging a wooden cocktail stick, or the back of a knife, to and fro over the surface before it sets. Place in the refrigerator until set and then cut into squares.
MAKES: 24 squares

Below: Quick and Easy Chocolates (left) and Chocolate Truffles (right)

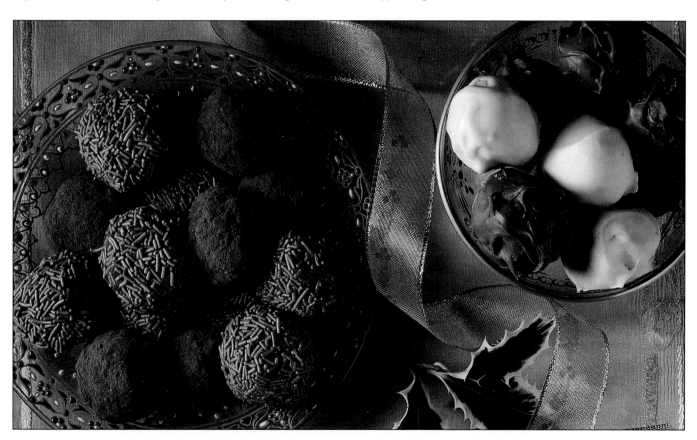

OILS AND VINEGARS

SUSAN BROOKES

Now that it is possible to buy herbs and fruits out of season, you can make flavoured oils and vinegars as Christmas gifts, even if you're too late to harvest them for free in your own garden. We grow a lot of herbs, so I usually have enough to preserve them in oils and vinegars. We grow our own raspberries too, but they often ripen all at once and it's hard enough to keep up with picking and freezing them, never mind making raspberry vinegar as well! However, it makes delicious salad dressings, and one year I did make it with our own home-grown fruit which I had in the freezer, and it worked perfectly well, if not better.

To make these oils and vinegars, it is worth investing in an inexpensive plastic funnel. This will make filling the bottles easier, especially if you intend making a lot.

You can buy very pretty clear or coloured glass bottles, or you can recycle household ones. Always make sure that you seal the tops well; a tightly fitting cork, pushed in firmly, should be sufficient. However, a little red sealing wax will be even better and will make the gift look more attractive. Don't use metal tops, especially for flavoured vinegars, as they may corrode.

BASIL OIL

Use an ordinary olive oil for this; not extra virgin. For each 600ml/1 pint oil you will need 6 tablespoons of chopped fresh basil leaves. Pound the basil in a mortar, or in a bowl with the end of a rolling pin. Add a little oil and pound again.

Mix in the remaining oil and pour into bottles, making sure that there is an even quantity of basil in each. Plug with a stopper and store for at least 2 weeks before using. During this time, shake the bottle every other day. If possible, leave on a sunny windowsill to infuse the flavour.

This oil will keep well without straining for up to 6 months. However, if you want to keep it longer, it should be strained through a fine sieve after a month. Drizzle it over tomato salads and pizzas, or use for making your own fresh pesto sauce.

WOK OIL

This is a popular gift with anyone who likes spicy foods or uses a wok for cooking. For each 600ml/1 pint sunflower oil add 3 or 4 dried red chillies, 2 or 3 cloves of garlic, peeled and halved, 8 juniper berries and 2 or 3 sprigs of rosemary.

Put all the ingredients in a large bottle and secure with a stopper. Store for at least 1 month before using, and shake the bottle occasionally. The oil can be kept for up to a year and will get progressively hotter as time passes, so use it with care. It is especially good in stir-fried oriental dishes, or for cooking Mexican food.

AROMATIC OIL

For this recipe use half ordinary olive oil and half sunflower oil. For each 600ml/1 pint of oil, add 4 or 5 sprigs of thyme, 3 or 4 sprigs of rosemary, 8 peppercorns and 4 or 5 cloves.

Pour into bottles and plug with stoppers. Stand on a sunny windowsill for at least 2 weeks before using, shaking from time to time. The scent improves with keeping.

RASPBERRY VINEGAR

For each 450g/1lb raspberries used, you will need 900ml/ 1½ pints white wine vinegar and 450g/1lb sugar.

Put the raspberries in a large saucepan with 600ml/ 1 pint water. Bring to the boil, then reduce the heat and simmer, uncovered, for 20 minutes. Remove from the heat and stir in the white wine vinegar and sugar. Continue to stir until the sugar has completely dissolved. Bring back to the boil, reduce the heat and simmer for 10 minutes. Strain through a fine sieve and bottle when cool.

TARRAGON VINEGAR

Chop and pound about 6 tablespoons of fresh tarragon leaves, and place them in a wide-necked bottle or jar.

Warm 600ml/1 pint cider vinegar or white wine vinegar to just below boiling point, and pour over the crushed leaves. Stopper the jar or bottle and shake well. Leave to infuse on a sunny windowsill or in a warm place for 2 weeks, shaking every day. Strain through a fine sieve and bottle in the usual way. If wished, add a sprig of fresh tarragon.

EDIBLE GIFTS

SUSAN BROOKES

CRANBERRY ORANGE SAUCE

200g/7oz sugar
150ml/¹/4 pint water
350g/12oz cranberries
juice of ¹/2 orange or 1 tablespoon orange liqueur

1 Put the sugar and water in a saucepan and add the cranberries. Bring slowly to the boil, stirring to dissolve the sugar. Reduce the heat and then simmer gently for a few minutes, until the cranberries have finished 'popping'.
2 Remove from the heat and set aside to cool. When just warm, stir in the orange juice or orange liqueur. Stir well and pour into warm, clean jars. Cover and store in a cool place. Eat within 2 weeks and store in the refrigerator after opening. Serve with turkey, chicken or ham.
MAKES: 2 × 450g/1lb jars

STUFFED DATES

If possible, try to find the big, juicy medjool dates for this delicious recipe. Make a slit along the side of each date lengthways and remove the stone. Fill the cavity with a strip of marzipan, either home-made or bought. Decorate each date with a small piece of candied fruit and then brush with warm honey to glaze.

BRANDIED KUMQUATS

450g/1lb kumquats
350g/12oz sugar
150ml/¹/4 pint brandy

1 Wash the kumquats and remove any stalks. Prick the skins in 2 or 3 places with a wooden cocktail stick. Put them in a saucepan with 300ml/¹/2 pint water and 115g/4oz of the sugar. Heat gently, stirring until the sugar dissolves, and then bring to the boil. Reduce the heat and poach for 5 minutes, until the skins are tender.
2 Drain the kumquats, reserving the poaching liquid. Divide the poached kumquats between 2 or 3 small clean jars. Measure out 150ml/¹/4 pint of the poaching liquid and pour it into a saucepan with the remaining sugar.
3 Stir over low heat to dissolve the sugar, and then bring to the boil. Boil for about 5 minutes, until syrupy. It will be ready when it forms a thread between 2 teaspoons. Set the syrup aside to cool a little and then measure it and add an equal amount of brandy. Mix well.
4 Pour the syrup over the fruit in the jars, and cover with lids. Store for up to 3 months. The kumquats will taste good after a few weeks so resist the temptation to eat them too early!
MAKES: 2-3 small jars

FIG AND ORANGE DIAMONDS

450g/1lb dried figs
115g/4oz candied peel
1 teaspoon ground cinnamon
juice of ¹/₂ orange
nuts or glacé fruit, to decorate
honey or apricot jam, to glaze

1 Cut the figs in half and place in a food processor, with the metal blade fitted. Add the candied peel and cinnamon, and process until finely chopped. Add enough orange juice to bind the mixture together into a ball.

2 Press this out to cover the base of a lined baking tin, and leave overnight to harden a little. Cut into diamond shapes and press a nut or glacé fruit on top of each one. Brush with a little warmed honey or apricot jam to glaze.
MAKES: 18

Below: Brandied Kumquats and Cranberry Orange Sauce

POMANDERS & POTTED CANDLES

MAGGIE COLVIN

These are so simple to make that even children can enjoy success; little boys, in particular, love stabbing the holes in the oranges. The only proviso is time; you need to make the pomanders at least eight weeks before Christmas to allow them to shrink.

POMANDERS

For each pomander you will need:
1 orange
2 thick elastic bands
a handful of cloves
0.5 metres/1ft 6in pretty Christmas ribbon
silver parcel string

Begin by wrapping the two elastic bands around the orange to divide it in half and then into equal quarters. Eventually these bands will make indentations in which the ribbon will sit securely.

Pierce the remaining skin of the orange with a cocktail stick or skewer, and stick the cloves, sharp end down, into the holes. Put aside in a warm place, such as an airing cupboard, for eight weeks. After that time, remove the elastic bands and tie the ribbon around the orange like a parcel. Thread a piece of silver parcel string under the bow and make a loop, so that the pomander can be hung from a coathanger or on the Christmas tree.

POTTED CANDLES

4 For variations on this theme, you can use a group of four candles, wrapped together with silver string, and a big fat 5cm/2-inch diameter red candle set in a nest of moss (available from specialist florists). Pack the edges with silver shells sprayed gold, and a few bits of spangled string.

1 Take a terracotta pot (even a plastic one will do), and gild it (see page 61). In addition, you will need some silver candles, a dry oasis cut to fit the pot, real moss (available from florists) and sprigs of real or fake berries.

3 For extra colour, arrange the sprigs of berries in an attractive border around the edge of the pot.

2 Cover the dry oasis with moss and insert the candles into the dry foam – you can wire them first if you wish but it is not strictly necessary.

GIFTS TO MAKE

MAGGIE COLVIN

Beginning with the easiest and quickest, each of these gift ideas can be styled to suit the recipient's taste. It is this flexibility of colour and styling that makes these presents so rewarding to create and give.

SILHOUETTES

You will need:

tracing paper
black marker pen
a frame with an oval mount (or a double frame if you prefer)

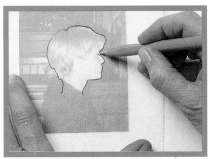

Take a profile photograph of your child, if possible to produce the right size for the frame. If you get it wrong, you can always have the print enlarged. Trace the outline of the profile, top and back or head and neck. Blacken in with the marker pen and run this through a photocopier or fax machine. Cut to

fit into the frame. In a double frame, making the profiles face each other is more visually satisfying than if facing the same way.

WASTEPAPER BASKET

You will need:

1 wastepaper basket
PVA glue
matt varnish
black emulsion paint
photocopied cuttings from an appropriate magazine or newpaper

As this was a present for a boy, I used *Beano* magazine cuttings. For an adult you might choose a newspaper, or pretty flowers for a girl. Cut out the paper bits and work out how you will assemble them. Paint the basket in emulsion and leave to dry. Brush PVA glue over the basket and stick the découpage (paper bits) in place. Leave to dry. Apply at least five coats of acrylic varnish. MDF wastepaper baskets are available by mail order (see page 143).

SECRET BOX

These boxes are available by mail order (see page 143) and make an original, decorative present which you can paint in any way you like. The blue box shown here is painted in 'Antique Blue' and then sponged with a little Indigo mixed in a glaze. The yellow box is painted in 'Parisian Yellow' and sponged with a little yellow oxide in a glaze. Both are painted inside in terracotta.

TISSUE BOX

Again, this shape is available in a kit by mail order (see page 143). In addition to the kit, which contains a pattern and acrylic paints, you will need the following:

a 2.5-4cm/1-1^1/$_2$-inch brush
a No. 6 flat brush
a No. 4 round brush
5mm/^{1}/$_4$-inch masking tape
fine sandpaper
a rubber

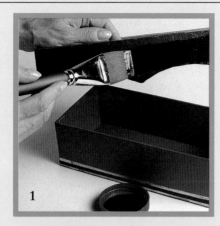

1

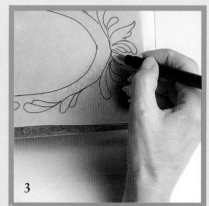

3

1 Paint the box terracotta all over. When dry, paint the sides of the box green. Paint a coat of crackle medium on the top of the lid.

2 Place the masking tape about 1cm/^{1}/$_2$-inch up from the base of the box and paint this space green. When dry, run the narrow masking tape round the middle of the green finger on the gold. Sponge the top of the lid with Antique White, using a natural sponge.

3 Transfer the pattern to the top of the box using tracing paper and art carbon.

4 Paint the tulips on the lid, using the No. 4 round brush, loaded with Alazarin Crimson, tip loaded with gold, and the comma scrolls using green paint, tip loaded in gold. Lightly sand the sides of the lid so a

2

little terracotta shows through the green. Rub off any chalk lines.

5 Antique the whole box using a soft cloth moistened in a solution of 1 part raw linseed oil to 3 parts white spirit. Rub this into a little artist's Burnt Umber oil paint and apply generously all over the box. Buff off any excess with a clean, soft cloth. Leave to dry for a few days before varnishing.

CANDLES AND CANDLESTICKS

MAGGIE COLVIN

MAKING WHITE CANDLES

You will need:

paraffin wax and Stearin
(or use ends of white candles)

a pencil

a mould or glass container

wick sustainers

wick

If wished, you can buy an introductory basic candle making kit (see page 143), which contains everything you need. The less expensive route is to buy wick by the yard together with some wick sustainers. Melt down your own half-burnt or stub ends of candles in a double boiler. When the wax has melted, carefully sift

Here are four easy ideas to arrange: floating candles in a small fluted bowl mixed with carnations; a jam jar filled with melted candlewax and decorated with gold cherubs and a silver-beaded rim; a wine glass filled with a ball-shaped candle; and a tiny gilded terracotta pot.

Opposite: A selection of wine and liqueur bottles, wine and sherry glasses used to hold candles can be decorated with silver spray and stick-on stars, or left clear and decorated with bows and tiny berry garlands.

out any old bits of wick. Take care: hot wax burns! Leave to cool for 5 minutes, until the wax looks cloudy but is still liquid.

Meanwhile, cut a piece of wick to the estimated required length of your candle and add 30cm/12 inches. Tie a wick sustainer to one end. This will anchor the wick to the bottom of the container. Set in place. Wind the other end around a pencil placed horizontally across the glass container. Pour the semi-cooled wax into the container and allow to set. Cut off any excess wick, leaving 1cm/^{1}/$_2$ inch at the top to light.

CANDLESTICKS AND CANDLE CONTAINERS

If you browse through the supermarket shelves you will find great scope for containers. Most glass jars are suitable, and small terracotta pots are also good, provided that you first seal their holes with some tape. To make them look different, you can gild them or spray them with gold paint before filling with wax.

CARDS AND WRAPS

MAGGIE COLVIN

If you are one of those 'squirrel' types who hoard old Christmas cards, this is the easy way to recycle them and even improve upon the original design.

POP-UP CARDS

You will need:

1 sheet flexible coloured card
some figures cut from old Christmas cards
glue
scissors
stick-on stars

1 Begin by cutting the coloured card into a rectangle, 15 x 25cm/6 x 10 inches.

2 Fold in two widthwise, and cut out the appropriate figures of your choice.

3 Cover the top insides of the card with a spattering of stars. Cut a strip of card, 2.5 x 10cm/1 x 4 inches, and fold it into a capital 'M' shape. Apply glue to the two outside edges of this shape. Fix one to the back of the card, and the other to the back of the cut-out figures. When the card is closed, the cardboard folds back on itself; when opened, the figures spring forwards.

AWKWARDLY SHAPED PRESENTS

These are often easier to wrap in fabric, such as gold lamé or gold net over a plain lining, or even using J-cloth material. Surprisingly, fabric often works out cheaper than conventional wrapping paper. The method is to wrap the present loosely in fabric and to secure the ends with elastic bands. Pretty up raw fabric edges with pinking shears.

BOTTLE WRAPS

Coloured tissue paper, wrapped around the bottle and teased out to form a flower shape, then topped with a flouncy Christmas ribbon, is not easy to improve upon. You can protect a wrapped bottle by placing it in a plastic cylinder (see far left).

STAMP DECORATIONS

These are useful items to keep in your Christmas props cupboard. They look particularly stunning in gold on coloured tissue paper. You can purchase stamps together with gold paint and application rollers from specialist suppliers (see page 143).

ALTERNATIVE WRAPPING PAPER

Huge savings can be made in the Christmas budget if you wrap presents with gold or silver sprayed newspaper. One spray can will cover at least sixteen large newspaper sheets, and the results are surprisingly lush. Ordinary brown paper can also look very smart teamed with gold ribbon and stamped with stars.

CHRISTMAS GIFT TAGS

Tags are expensive to buy, and I always cut my own out of old Christmas cards or stiff card: gold or silver one side and plain white on the reverse. Use pinking shears for a plain rectangular shape; or cut out snowmen, star, bell and Christmas tree shapes. It may be helpful to make a template first. Make holes for the ribbon with an ordinary office hole puncher.

GIFT BOXES AND BASKETS

MAGGIE COLVIN

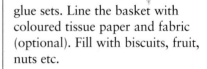

Presentation is all-important, and home-made chocolates lushly packaged in a silk-covered box can be made to look fit for a king. Your basic ingredients need not cost a penny. The ice-cream boxes shown here are off the supermarket shelves, and the baskets the remains of bouquets given by kind friends. Your only necessary investment may be a roll of pretty ribbon.

DECORATING BASKETS

You will need:

baskets
gold aerosol spray
dressmakers' pins
sellotape
coloured tissue paper
glue
ribbon or star-spangled wire

First, spray your basket gold. When dry, cut a length of ribbon to encircle the basket handle. Fix one end to where the handle joins the basket with sellotape. Wrap the ribbon around the handle and fix at the other side by winding the ribbon onto itself and making a neat knot. Make two bows. For perfect bows, see the bow-maker method opposite. Glue the ribbons in place and hold with dressmakers' pins until the glue sets. Line the basket with coloured tissue paper and fabric (optional). Fill with biscuits, fruit, nuts etc.

TRUFFLES SWEET BOX

You will need:

a small cardboard box
scraps of silk material
ribbon
fabric glue
coloured tissue paper
dressmakers' pins
few sheets of kitchen roll

Measure the width of the lid and the distance between the back outside edge and inside lid edge of the box. Cut a piece of silk fabric to these dimensions, adding 2.5cm/1 inch for 1cm/$^{1}/_{2}$-inch turn-ins. Cut two sheets of kitchen roll to the exact size of the

lid and stick in place to create a cushioned effect. Wrap the silk around the box lid, turning under the raw edges. Glue them on to the lid. Use dressmakers' pins to hold as it dries. Line the base of the box in the same way or use stick-on green felt. Cut a piece of ribbon to cover and wrap around the outside edges of the box. Either use a ribbon the exact depth of the box or butt two ribbons on to each other. Glue the raw end of the ribbon under, and overlap a corner of the box with the other end and glue in place. Make sure the turned edges sit exactly in line with the corner (see photo). Line the inside of the box with tissue paper, and arrange the chocolates inside. As a final touch, wrap the box with a ribbon tied in a bow.

MAKING BOWS

2 Take the tail of ribbon that will secure the cross-over, under all the loops.

For perfect bows of all sizes, it is worth investing in this bow maker (for stockists, see page 143).

1 With right side of ribbon facing out, wind it around the poles as many times as the number of loops required. Make sure the tails are about the same length. Cross over the tails, keeping the crossing point central.

3 Bring it back round on itself, over the top and back to the other tail, to encircle all the loops, keeping it in a central position.

4 Tie the tails in a knot, adjusting them to make sure that the right side faces to the front of the bow before pulling tight. Remove the bow from the poles and trim the tails to the required length.

PART THREE

CREATIVE CHRISTMAS

Putting up decorations dates back to pagan mid-winter festivals when evergreens were hung for good luck. We still deck out our homes with branches of fir and holly as well as paper and tinsel decorations. Maggie Colvin has original and creative ideas for making your house look festive, creating your own table centrepieces and wreaths, and even making your own stylish Christmas tree decorations and crackers.

TREE DECORATIONS

MAGGIE COLVIN

In a perfect world, Mrs Perfect confines her tree to a well defined colour scheme and, of course, this works. However, in the real world, you have accrued a boxful of decorations from over the years, and these present a visual mish mash. It needs ruthless editing, revamping and adding to – all on a tight budget. Here are some quick, simple and inexpensive ideas which you can colour to match your existing stock.

GILDING SHELLS

Pick raw materials off the beach. To gild the shells, you can use either a gilding cream, which you simply brush on with a thick stencil brush, or Dutch metal and some Wondersize and glue (for stockists, see page 143).

Gold was one of the presents given to the baby Jesus so you can't go wrong if you choose a predominantly gold colour scheme.

Make sure the item you are gilding is dust-free and dry. Paint with a liberal coat of the size and wait for it to go tacky; this takes about 5 minutes, and the size turns from a pale blue to a lighter shade as it dries. Carefully lift the Dutch metal from its paper leaf backing and place over the shell. Pat it and smooth it flat, allowing it to penetrate the grooves of the shell. When adding a second piece, overlap at the joins. You will find that Dutch metal is tougher than it looks. Brush off any flaky bits and glue some ribbon folded in two to the inside of the shell.

RECYCLING LAST YEAR'S BAUBLES

Baubles are prone to chip, and often you unpack them to find that the hooks have been left on last year's tree! To revamp them, you need the following:

some glitzy material (like gold lamé or gold net)
pinking shears
spangly star wire
elastic bands
gold parcel string

With the pinking shears, cut a piece of fabric about 20cm/8 inches square – the exact size depends on the size of the bauble. Wrap the fabric around the bauble to enclose it. Use a lining if you choose net. Secure the fabric with an elastic band, and then trim the fabric frill with pinking shears to cut away the corners. Wrap the spangly star wire round the elastic band to hide it. Finally, tie round the gold string to make a hook for hanging the bauble on the tree.

MAKING PAPER HEARTS

Depending on how strong a paper you choose to use, you can vary the size of these hearts. Hang them on the tree, filled with sweets or chocolates. Apart from paper, you need tartan ribbon, scissors and a small staple gun.

Fold in two across the middle to create a square. Fold the seam up and under.

3 Cut along the pencil line and open up the heart. Staple the seam to the back of the heart.

1 Draw a rectangle, which should be a double square size, e.g. the one shown is 20cm/ 8 inches by 10cm/4 inches, and then add 1cm/½ inch to its length.

2 Next fold the square diagonally at a 45-degree angle, and draw a half heart shape lightly in pencil.

4 Make a small bow and cut a second piece of ribbon, about 20cm/8 inches long, to make the handle. Fold this in two and staple one end to the back of the heart, and the other to the front back. Staple the bow to the middle of the heart as shown.

FESTIVE RINGS

To make these, you will need:

a collection of curtain rings, any size and any colour

sellotape

gold thread or parcel string

small stars (optional extras)

narrow ribbons to complement your tree decorations

Cut a piece of ribbon, about 50cm/20 inches long – the exact size depends on the size of your curtain ring, so you will need to experiment. Secure one end with sellotape to the curtain ring, butting on to the hook. Wrap the ribbon around the ring, overlapping marginally so that the curtain hook is covered completely – unless, of course, the ring is brass and you want the gold to show through. When you get back to your starting point, wrap the ribbon around the sellotape for extra staying power and thread the ribbon through the hook. Knot to keep it from slipping. Tie a bow and secure this to the curtain hook with the parcel thread. Attach a gold star to hang inside the ring, and make a loop with the parcel thread to hang off the tree.

Right: To make the most stylish impact, stick to a consistent colour scheme like this one in red, green and gold.

ALTERNATIVE TREES AND CRACKERS

Here are two stylish alternatives to the traditional festive conifer, and they are both quick and easy to arrange.

CONICAL TREE

You will need the following:

a conical wire shape (sold by some florists)
4 or 5 sheets of coloured tissue paper
sellotape
a set of white Christmas tree lights

Gently place the tissue paper inside and up against the conical shape as if to line it. Crease the paper slightly to bend around corners. Try not to overlap corners too overtly, as you want to maintain consistent translucency. Tape the end loop of the lights to the inside top of the cone, and wind the lights within the spiral shape, spacing them evenly.

STICK TREE

You will need the following:

a spiral twizzle stick (available from specialist garden shops)
a flower pot, preferably ready gilded
a bag of Polyfilla
8 or 9 decorations, with a strong graphic shape and shiny texture
strong tape
cardboard, cut to fit base of pot
moss

If necessary, begin by gilding the pot (see page 61). Cover the inside base with the round piece of cardboard; draw around the pot to establish the size and then undercut by the thickness of the pot. Make up the Polyfilla, following the manufacturer's instructions. Use to fill the pot and stick the spiral twizzle stick into the middle. Wedge it upright with strong tape until the Polyfilla dries, about 1 hour. Hide the Polyfilla with a top layer of moss. Attach the decorations sparingly.

MAKING CHRISTMAS CRACKERS

They may be decorated in a thousand different ways, but below the foil, tinsel, ribbons and trims, all crackers are made using this basic technique. Although you can buy complete cracker kits, the most cost-effective method I have found is to buy a bunch of basic snappers and enjoy the challenge of making your own nutty riddles, chocolate fillers and trimmings.

You will need the following:

flexible white card

wrapping paper

snappers

gold thread

scissors

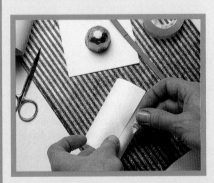

1 Cut three rectangles from the white flexible card. The largest middle section should be 13cm/5 inches by 20cm/8 inches, and the outer sections both 8cm/3 inches but the same width as the middle piece. Roll the rectangles into tubes, slightly overlapping the

edges by equal amounts, and secure with sellotape. Cut the wrapping paper into one rectangle, 25cm/10 inches wide by 36cm/14 inches long.

2 Butt the tubes together and slot a snapper inside. Wrap the wrapping paper around all three and secure with sellotape.

3 Wind a length of gold thread between each tube, ruching the wrapping paper in between the tube joins and tie securely. Glue on the finishing touches.

DECORATING ROOMS FOR CHRISTMAS

There is no doubt that some rooms adapt more easily than others to a Christmas look. Rooms decorated in dark colours, greens and crimsons, or even terracotta and browns, make the switch far easier than, say, a pale peach, yellow or leafy green room. So before you begin to think of ingredients to add to the room, consider first what to take out. I remove or hide all summery fabrics and pale colours, and I even change the tablecloths and remove paintings of summer beach scenes.

Tartan rugs have great power to transform and can be used to hide flowery, chintzy sofa covers. They evoke a subtle suggestion of snow on the Scottish Highlands, while you sit with your family and friends celebrating in front of a roaring fire. If you happen to have the wrong coloured lampshades, tartan wrapping paper, cut to fit around a shade, will provide an instant disguise to match the rugs.

DECORATING THE FIREPLACE

Despite all the architectural upheavals of this century, the fireplace has retained its position as the heart of the home. Clearly, decorating the fireplace is priority number one. To realise the full visual potential of a Victorian fireplace, like the one shown opposite, I always like to clear the mantelpiece completely of any photographs, clocks, china figures and all the usual clutter.

Next I set about making a garland; mine is a combination of real and fake. The main bulk is fake, a long swag of conifer and holly which I wind around each other and hang off the mantelpiece secured with green tape. Into this I weave branches of real holly, masses of ivy and any other branches laden with berries that I can find. Surprisingly, most evergreens are pretty hardy, and even in a centrally heated house, they should last eight to ten days; long enough to see you into the New Year before wilting.

To decorate the mantelshelf, I round up every candlestick in the house and place them on top, together with round candles in tall-stemmed wine glasses and a row of nightlights as an outside star-studded edge.

I like to hang my Christmas cards from picture bows or real bows. Of course, you can tie your own bows (see page 57 for instructions).

WORTHWHILE INVESTMENTS

Certain decorations never go out of fashion and won't break. Invaluable investments, in my opinion, include a round or rectangular Christmas cloth. Edged with real ivy and secured with dressmakers' pins, this table (opposite) is loaded with candlesticks collected specially for Christmas. Many department stores sell a great range of Christmas fabrics. Although it is comparatively expensive, crimply wired ribbon is worth buying, and as it comes ready creased it does not require ironing.

If you remove your cushion covers to their naked calico, you can tie them up like presents using the ribbon. Keep bows ready tied for next year. A glamorous pair of sconces and some fake garlands of Christmas flowers always look

opulent and extremely festive, especially when finished with tartan bows (see below).

DRIED FLOWER ARRANGEMENTS

You will need the following:

a small terracotta pot
a dozen dried rose heads
Polyfilla
raffia
glue
a bunch of wheat or dried lavender
bits of moss

Fill the hole in the base of the pot with a piece of cardboard cut to fit inside. Fill to about 2.5cm/1 inch of the top with Polyfilla. Bunch the wheat or lavender together, making sure that the heads line up.

Place in the middle of the pot and secure with masking tape as the Polyfilla sets. This takes at least 1 hour, depending on room temperature. Cover the Polyfilla with moss and a line of dried rose heads, using a strong glue or, better still, a glue gun. For extra finish, wrap some raffia around the pot, well below the top as shown.

MAKING A SIMPLE WREATH

WREATH FOR THE FRONT DOOR

You will need the following:

a 75cm/30-inch diameter moss
or wire frame to which you wire
your own moss

florist's wire

blue spruce

ivy

variegated holly

eucalyptus

apples, sprayed gold (optional)

fir cones

cinnamon parcels

chestnuts or walnuts

Cut the greenery into manageable 13cm/5-inch long pieces, and bind them into small bunches. Twist the florist's wire around the base of each bunch, and push each diagonally into the frame. Twist some wire around the fir cones and cinnamon parcels and push into the arrangement. Wire the nuts by piercing the bases and securing them with glue.

To wire the apples, insert two pieces of wire at right angles to each other, and twist the ends together underneath each apple. If wished, tie on a bow and attach it to the wreath with florist's wire.

MAKING INDOOR WREATHS

This indoor wreath is simple to make and far easier to arrange than the outdoor version. It is based on twigs woven into a circle. These wreaths can be bought from most leading florists. In addition, you will need the following:

3 or 4 strands of variegated ivy
florist's wire
fir cones
gold spray
cinnamon parcels
a few sprigs of greenery with berries

2 Wire up the cinnamon parcels and fir cones, and then attach these to the wreath.

3 Trim any wayward strands of greenery to create a tidy circle.

4 Tie a bow, using gilt-edged wire ribbon, and attach it to the base with florist's wire.

1 Start by twisting the ivy strands around the wreath, tucking the ends under a twig and securing the other end with florist's wire. Spray the fir cones lightly with gold paint and leave to dry.

THE CENTRE OF ATTRACTION

The key to successful table decorations is to combine two or three simple elements and use them in abundance as opposed to an unco-ordinated varied mixture. The shape of the arrangement should reflect the shape of the table's surface.

POTTED CANDLESTICK ON A PLATTER

You will need the following:

| 8 or 9 fir cones |
| 2 bows |
| 2 or 3 parcels of cinnamon sticks |
| 2 or 3 strands of real ivy |
| a wooden platter |
| a candle in a glass pot |

Begin by making the cinnamon parcels, about 4 sticks in a pack. Wrap them with silver string. Place the candle in the centre of the platter. Next arrange the fir cones (you can spray these with gold or silver first, if wished). Lay 2 or 3 cinnamon parcels, evenly dispersed, on top. Encircle the platter with ivy – stick the ends in place if they spring out. Finally, place the bows, facing outwards, directly opposite each other.

TANGERINE PLATTER

You will need the following:

| 1 gold platter |
| about 16 tangerines with leaves still attached |
| about 12 walnuts |
| Dutch metal leaf |
| Wondersize (see page 143) |

Begin by gilding the walnuts (see page 61). Pile the tangerines on to the platter, arranging the leaves prettily. Place the walnuts to sit, if possible, between 2 leaves to accentuate the contrast between the gold and dark green.

CANDLES AND FRESH GREENERY

You will need the following:

circular oasis (available from specialist florists)

4 candles, at least 25-30cm/ 10-12 inches tall

about 16 sprigs of evergreen leaves and viburnum or gypsophilla

1 metre/3 feet of translucent wired ribbon

Begin by positioning the candles to make a perfect square within the round oasis, and stand it in a plastic trough. Arrange the greenery in between the candles. Add some viburnum or gypsophilla flowers, to contrast with the dark leaves. Make sure that the oasis is hidden completely by foliage. Finally twist the ribbon around the outside edge of the arrangement in order to hide any visible parts of the plastic trough.

TREATS FOR THE TABLE

OPULENT SETTING

(below)

Predominantly a scheme in blue and gold, the blue side plate with a gold trim is encircled in ruched gold crinkly ribbon and sits on a gold platter. The central arrangement has four tall blue fluted glasses, precisely placed to form a square. Each glass is filled with water and contains a floating flower-shaped candle and is linked to its neighbour by a beaded chain of gold stars.

GREEN AND RED SETTING

(left)

This is a more traditional colour scheme of green and red set against a tartan tablecloth. A garland of berries placed on a stemmed vase encircles the red candle, and the matching napkin slots into a smaller version of the same garland. All these ingredients are fake (which does not make them any less stunning to look at), but an effective contrast is provided by the bed of natural conifer branches which encircle each dinner plate.

THEATRICAL SETTING

(right)

For a frothy-looking round table, I circle it with swags of white net on to which are stapled little gold stars. What remains of the packet of gold stars gets sprinkled over a white linen cloth. You can purchase white and gold star plates, and starred glasses. In the centre of the table is an arrangement of lush white lilies, while evergreens, picked from the garden, sit in an oasis secured to a gilded flower basket. The gold star napkin rings are Christmas tree decorations adapted with gold ribbon which threads through the star and ties at the back of the folded napkin.

PART FOUR

CHEERS!

Carefree Christmas drinking calls for planning as much as any other part of the festive season. You can order and buy wines and spirits in advance and avoid the last-minute panic buying in your local supermarket or off-licence. Just sit down and work out what you'll need, not forgetting soft drinks for drivers and children. In this chapter, Charles Metcalfe will lead you through the maze of what to buy, which wines go with which foods, and how to make some delicious punches and party drinks, both alcoholic and non-alcoholic.

BUYING WINES

CHARLES METCALFE

Lots of the top bargains for Christmas drinking will be found on the shelves of off-licences and supermarkets. Keep watching **This Morning** for my top retail tips! However, if you're willing to plan ahead just that little bit more, there are two other ways of doing your Christmas drinks shopping. Either you can shop from the comfort of your favourite chair by mail-order, or, and I have to include this these days, you can go on a cross-Channel trip.

Let's take the second way first. A cross-Channel trip will need more planning, but can provide an enjoyable day out (or even a weekend) in France, with the saving on the drink paying for the cost of the trip. However, do not be tempted to bring back drink for friends and associates, even if you have the money from them in advance. If you want to go with a couple of friends (who are also buying drink) in a hired van and split the costs of the trip, fine, but going on your own and bringing back alcoholic drinks for someone else is against the law.

Anyway, you can bring back such substantial amounts of drink from France, minus the punishing duty we pay on wine bought over here, that it really is not worth contemplating turning to a life of crime! Before raising a Customs man's eyebrow, you can bring in ten dozen bottles of wine (of which up to 80 litres, i.e. 106 bottles, can be sparkling), thirteen bottles of spirits, twenty-seven bottles of fortified wine and 110 litres of beer. (Note: this

is correct at time of going to press.) If that isn't enough to keep Christmas nicely celebrated with a few friends and relations, you may have an alcohol problem!

Buying beer and spirits from French supermarkets is all well and good. You can go for your favourite names, and the prices are sigificantly cheaper than in the UK. However, wine is a lottery. French supermarkets are much less quality-conscious than their British counterparts, as they buy on price. You will scoop an occasional super-bargain, but you'll inevitably bring back dodgy

plonk as well. In Calais, Boulogne and Dunquerque, however, the northern supermarket chain of PG does better than most. Best of all, though, are Sainsbury and Tesco. Yes, Sainsbury have opened a big wine and beer shop in the Mammouth shopping precinct near Calais, and there's a huge Tesco store in the Cité de l'Europe shopping centre by the French exit from the Channel Tunnel.

Elsewhere, the wise alternative to the many French supermarkets is wine shops, far thinner on the ground in France, since many Frenchmen buy direct from the grower. Turn to pages 142-143 at the back of this book for my list of top shops.

WINE BY MAIL ORDER

Almost everyone will supply wine by mail (even Marks & Spencer, Tesco, Waitrose and Sainsbury). It's the best way to shop for anyone who hates carrying cases of wine, and if you're elderly or have back problems, it makes good sense. Most of Britain's best wine merchants have beautifully produced, informative wine lists.

Phone for a list, then settle down to browse, and make sure that you order before the Christmas deadline for delivery. Order two or more cases and you'll often get free delivery (unless you live on an off-shore island), but this varies. Unless you're blessed with an especially good local wine merchant, buying wine by mail order usually offers a bigger choice than from local shops. You will find terrific wines from unexpected places at some merchants who specialize in wines from particular regions. If you're not sure when you first see a list, order a mixed case and try those before buying caseloads. Turn to pages 142-143 for more information.

CHAMPAGNE AND FIZZ

You know you want some sparkling wine, but what should you choose? Perhaps you had Champagne last time, and it seemed very good value until the stomach-ache the morning after. Maybe you should pay a little bit more this time. Or maybe you should forget Champagne altogether, and buy some other type of sparkling wine. Australia, California, England, Germany, Italy, the Loire, New Zealand, South Africa or Spain? Everyone's making it, so where do you start?

First of all, what do you want the fizz for? Is it a special bottle or two to celebrate the start of your Christmas dinner, for family only? Or is it to serve to friends and neighbours at your Boxing Day party? If it's for the celebration, then it's worth buying the best you can afford, and that probably means Champagne. If it's to be party bubbly, Champagne will be a waste of money. What you really need is my international guide to sparkling wines, country by country.

France

Champagne: The world's most famous fizz region. Champagne still makes the best sparkling wines in the world, but the best are very expensive. Buy a bottle of Moet & Chandon's Dom Perignon or vintage Krug, and you will be in umpteenth heaven, but try Bloggitts special offer cheapo brand, and you may well have stomach-ache! With any Champagne under £10, buy a bottle first to make sure you like it before you buy a lot. The secret of Champagne's success is three excellent grape varieties (Chardonnay, Pinot Noir and Pinot Meunier), a long growing season, and very skilful blending of large batches of wine of different character.

Loire: The other main source of French fizz, with production centred round the city of Saumur. Most is made from the Chenin Blanc grape, and has a crisp, green appley flavour, darkening to honey and toast as it ages in the bottle. Sparkling Vouvray can be among the Loire's best fizz. Otherwise, Saumur Mousseux and Crémant de Loire (slightly superior in quality) are the most widely seen names.

Burgundy: Sparkling wine from Burgundy is called 'Crémant de Bourgogne', and is usually made from Chardonnay. It is usually about half the price of Champagne and simpler in flavour, but made from riper grapes, so less acid – and good for parties.

England

Well, why not? We have a northerly climate like Champagne. Even more northerly, in fact. And that's the general problem for English vineyards: it's hard for us to get the grapes ripe. However, sparkling wine has to have pretty high acidity, so unripe grapes matter less for fizz than for table wines. And English sparklers are pretty good. Try them.

Germany

'Sekt' is what the Germans call their bubbly. By far the best is made from German Riesling grapes. So look for Riesling on the label; it's crisp, appley, honeyed bubbly.

Italy

Most Italian fizz comes from the cooler north of the country. Asti, from Piedmont, is all sweetness, froth and fun; Prosecco, from the Veneto, is light and refreshing; and Franciacorta, from Lombardy, is softer and richer. Some good and inexpensive Chardonnay bubblies ('Spumante' is the Italian word) are available.

Spain

'Cava', Spain's home-grown version of Champagne, is becoming more and more popular in Britain. Most is made near Barcelona, in Catalonia, from three rather bland Spanish grapes, Macabeo, Parellada and Xarello. It's best drunk young and fresh, so avoid anything that is obviously more than two years old.

Australia

We drink more and more beaut Ozzie bubbly over here; it's cheap, tasty and doesn't give you stomach-cramps. The cheapest wines are light and easy-drinking, then come wines between £6 and £8 that really show the fruity side of

Australia, and finally a few more expensive, complex wines around the £10 mark that really come near the quality of Champagne. Most of the middle and upper bracket wines are made from Chardonnay and Pinot Noir grape varieties.

California

It's quite pricey, California fizz, and only the top ones are really worth the money. Chardonnay and Pinot Noir again, but, with rare exceptions, you'd be better off with other New World bubbly.

New Zealand

Possibly this is the one country that has the potential to rival Champagne. The Kiwis use the classic Champagne grapes, the same production methods, and also advice from wine experts from Champagne. The climate is mild, and rainfall is similar to that of northern Europe. The soils are different from Champagne's chalk, but New Zealand fizz gets better every year. And, best of all, it's not expensive.

South Africa

South African sparklers have hit Britain with a resounding pop in the last couple of years. They've sold too much, in fact, and quality has fallen a little. However, if they organise themselves better, you should look out for gentle, malty sparklers made from Pinot Noir and Chardonnay.

WHITE WINES

I'm going to go through the world's wines by grape variety. Knowing your grapes is one of the best ways to find your way round the wine shelves. Most wines are labelled with the name of the grape(s) from which they are made. It's the flavours of these grapes, together with the local climate and winemaking, that give a wine a particular taste.

Chardonnay

Still the world's sexiest grape (and it's absolutely fabulous with smoked salmon!). Everyone wants to plant it, make wine out of it and cash in on the Chardonnay reputation. It's the only grape in the great white Burgundies and indispensable in the trio of grapes that make up the blend of Champagne. However, it's in Australia, New Zealand, South Africa and even the south of France that Chardonnay is grabbing the headlines at the moment. It's from there that its easy, buttery style, pineapple smoothed over with a little cream, perhaps rounded out with some vanilla oak flavour, has won it converts by the thousand.

Chenin blanc

Chenin Blanc can make some of the world's best sweet white wines, both at its home in the Loire in good years, and down in South Africa in most years. They're not as super-sweet as Sauternes and Barsac from Bordeaux, so go well with fresh fruit, if you fancy giving your digestive system a rest after Christmas and mince pies! The names to look for in the Loire are Coteaux du Layon, Bonnezeaux, Quarts de Chaume and Vouvray Moelleux. Most of the Loire's fizz is also made from (dry) Chenin Blanc.

Gewurztraminer

One of the most aromatic of white grapes, with scents of rose-petals and lychees, but, strangely enough, what Gewurztraminer goes with best is cheese! It's delicious as an aperitif, too. Most Gewurztraminers come from Alsace in northern France, but some are made in Germany, Austria, South Africa, Australia and New Zealand.

Muscat

This is the wine for Christmas pudding! Specifically, Asti, with its cascade of frothy sweetness, but other Muscats, such as Muscat de Beaumes-de-Venise, Muscat de Rivesaltes and Rutherglen Liqueur Muscat are also terrific, although richer and more alcoholic. Most Muscats are made sweet, and go brilliantly with chocolate, orange or almond flavoured desserts, but there are some dry ones as well, particularly from Alsace. Asti and Moscato Spumante are relatively low in alcohol.

Pinot blanc

Not the most characterful member of the Pinot family, but honeyed, gentle drinking from Alsace, Italy (as Pinot Bianco) and Weissburgunder in Germany and Austria. This is good as a dry white wine for beginners!

Pinot gris

Any Frenchman from Alsace will tell you that Pinot Gris Vendange Tardive is the only thing to drink with foie gras. This rich, sweetish, honeyed, intriguingly flavoured wine tastes wonderful with duck or goose liver (so is Sauternes from Bordeaux). Alsace Pinot Gris (sometimes called Tokay-Pinot Gris) can be dry too, and Pinot Gris also appears in Germany as Rulander and in Italy as Pinot Grigio. Outside Alsace, the wines are usually light, tangy and swiggable.

Riesling

A light and off-dry German Riesling Kabinett or Spatlese is a lovely bottle for drinking, well, just by itself. Mid-afternoon, or taken as an aperitif before dinner, German Riesling is one of the world's most delicious wines, with a refreshing balance between ripe fruit and crisp acidity. Riesling is grown all over the world, and is made into wines from tooth-curdlingly dry to opulently sweet. In Germany and Austria, it will be sweet or sweetish unless it says *trocken* (dry) or *halbtrocken* (off-dry)

on the label. In other countries, it will probably be dry or almost dry unless it says Late Harvest (Vendange Tardive). The flavours run from crisp apples, through honey and strawberries and cream, to toasty lime. Some more excellent Rieslings are made in Alsace (France), Australia, New Zealand, South Africa and California.

Sauvignon blanc

As simple Bordeaux Sauvignon Blanc, this is one of the easiest and most satisfactory matches with a whole range of simple fish dishes. Sauvignon Blanc is almost always dry, crisp and grassy, with different intensity of flavour found in different places. In the eastern Loire (Sancerre and Pouilly Fumé) and New Zealand, it is very aromatic, alive with scents of ripe gooseberries, exotic fruits and freshly cut grass. In Bordeaux and South Africa, the flavours are gentler.

Semillon

This is the other great wine style for duck or goose liver, and a host of different puds. Anything made with apple, pineapple, strawberries, peaches or cream is glorious with the sweet wines of Sauternes and Barsac (both made from Semillon). As an Australian dry white, Semillon makes concentrated wines tasting of toast and lime.

RED WINES

Let's turn our attention to red wines. You may already know what you like to drink with what at Christmas: "We always have Nuits-St-Georges with the turkey", that sort of thing. But you do have to think about which red wines go with which foods, because most red wines need food to taste at their best (as opposed to white wines, which slip down easily without).

As with whites, I'm going to describe the world's red wine styles by grape.

Cabernet Sauvignon

If you're thinking of a roast goose for your Christmas dinner, red Bordeaux is the perfect wine. It is also very good with roast lamb and venison dishes. Cabernet Sauvignon plays the leading role in most classic clarets, but has also travelled round the world and put down roots in countries as far apart as Austria and Australia. Depending on the warmth of the climate, Cabernet Sauvignon can make wines from leafy and herbaceous to ripely blackcurranty and tarry. In Bordeaux, Cabernet Sauvignon makes tough, long-lived wines with grassy, blackcurrant flavours, almost always mixed with Merlot, and often with Cabernet Franc and Petit Verdot too. In other countries, Cabernet Sauvignon often performs solo: you'll see its name on bottles from Australia, Bulgaria, California, Chile, Italy, Romania, South Africa and Spain.

Gamay

Gamay is the gentle gulper of Beaujolais, and terrific with roast beef or ham. In Beaujolais, Gamay can make the lightest of scented, pastilley reds,

WHICH WINES WITH WHICH FOODS?	
Turkey:	Syrah
Goose:	Cabernet Sauvignon
Beef:	Gamay
Lamb:	Cabernet Sauvignon, Tempranillo
Duck:	Nebbiolo
Pheasant:	Syrah, Sangiovese, Pinot Noir, Syrah
Venison:	Cabernet Sauvignon, Pinot Noir, Syrah
Ham:	Gamay
Cheese:	Pinot Noir, Sangiovese

or rich, plummy wines from some of the individual villages such as Moulin à Vent and Morgon.

Merlot

Merlot is the wine to go for with a recipe combining meat with some sweetness. It is the smoothie of the Bordeaux bunch, honeyed, raisiny and ripe even in the mild climate of south-western France. It makes rich, ripe, honeyed reds under its own name all over the world. In cooler climates, such as north-eastern Italy and Hungary, Merlot makes light, attractive, faintly grassy reds.

Nebbiolo

Nebbiolo is the grape of Barolo and Barbaresco, two of Italy's great red wines. It's another powerful savoury red, good with game dishes, brilliant with duck, and grown almost only in Piemonte, in the north-west of Italy. The best Barolos and Barbarescos can have lovely raspberry fruitiness, and the perfumes of truffles, malt and violets.

Pinot Noir

If you're a lover of game, feathered or furred, Pinot Noir is one of the likeliest wines as an accompaniment. It's the grape of red Burgundy (and also one of the two main grapes in Champagne), and can make some of the most interesting and complex reds in the world. Pheasant, hare, venison and wild boar are all good matches for Pinot Noir, whether it is grown in Burgundy or elsewhere. It's also a much better match for most cheeses

Hermitage, Cote Rotie, Crozes-Hermitage, St Joseph and Cornas are the local Syrah-based wines there. When it's young, Syrah/Shiraz delivers bold, clear raspberry fruit, and these darken with age and maturity to leathery, gamey complexity.

Tempranillo

The most important grape in Rioja, and brilliant with roast lamb. It's Spanish through and through, and turns up in Navarra, Aragon, Ribera del Duero, La Mancha, Valdepenas and throughout Catalonia. Tempranillo wines have plummy fruit when young, turning to savoury, wild strawberry scents with age in barrel and bottle.

Zinfandel

A real California super-star and, as a red, the perfect wine for hamburgers! Zinfandel is made into every shade and style of wine imaginable, from pale pink, off-dry 'White Zinfandel' to rich, spicy reds, full of berry fruitiness.

FORTIFIED WINES

Port, sherry, Madeira and the fortified Muscats from the south of France, which I referred to in the Muscat grape entry, are all what is known as 'fortified' wines. This means that at some stage in their production alcohol is added to them, which increases their strength. Originally, this was to make them more stable for primitive transport conditions. Now, this addition of alcohol has become part of the wines' style. Let me give you a quick run-down on the different types.

than claret. Young Burgundy is fresh and fruity (raspberry, strawberry or plum), with quite high tannin. As Burgundy matures, it becomes more savoury and complex, with flavours of mushroom, woodsmoke, pheasant prunes, cream and even of rotting vegetables. Pinot Noir makes light reds in Alsace, Germany, Switzerland, the Loire and north-east Italy.

Sangiovese

Sangiovese is another grape for savoury reds, good with game dishes and cheeses. It's the grape of Tuscany, and mainly responsible for Chianti (in all its forms) and Brunello di Montalcino. The best of these are rich and plummy when young, developing a cedary flavour with age.

Syrah

Aussie Shiraz is the perfect turkey wine. Shiraz (or Syrah, as it's known in France) is also good with wild duck, pheasant, partridge, venison and wild boar. However, you won't often see 'Syrah' printed on Rhone wine labels.

Port

This comes in a bewildering variety of styles. It is made from grapes grown in the dramatically steep vineyards around the Douro river, four hours inland from Oporto in northern Portugal. During the fermentation of the grape-juice, alcohol is added to kill the yeast and stop the fermentation. This means that some of the grape sugar is left in the finished port, unfermented, so port is always sweet. It has to be aged for at least two years before it is sold. Some ports are aged for much longer.

White Port: This port is made from white grapes only. It is rather coarse and alcoholic, and best drunk with tonic water, ice and a slice of lemon.

Tawny Port: Cheap tawny is watered-down, or filtered, red port, and doesn't taste of much at all. Aged tawny (ten, twenty, thirty or forty years old) is one of the most delicious ports of all. It's aged in wooden vats until sold, a pale, tawny colour, with a marvellous nut and fig fragrance. It is the best wine for serving with Stilton.

Ruby Port: This is basic red port, probably matured for little more than the minimum three years. 'Premium' ruby takes in most of the famous port brands, and should be a good fruity drink, which it sometimes is.

Vintage Character Port: This is really up-market ruby port.

Late-bottled Port: A blend of ruby matured for a little longer than the minimum length of time before bottling and sale. 'Late-bottled Vintage' (or LBV) is the same port, but from a particular year.

Vintage Port: Tip-top quality port, from a particularly good vintage, bottled after only two years in a vat. The rest of the maturation is in the bottle, and takes fifteen to twenty-five years, depending on the vintage.

Single Quinta Port: Vintage port from a lesser year, bottled after only two years in the vat, and from a single quinta (estate). It is less expensive than, but similar in style to, real vintage port.

Sherry

Sherry comes from the south-west corner of Spain near Cadiz, and is made in three towns, Jerez de la Frontera, Sanlucar de Barrameda and Puerto de Santa Maria. It starts life as a very boring dry white wine, and is fortified after fermentation. The maturation after the alcohol has been added then determines the sherry's final flavour. All sherry starts dry but is often sweetened for export. Like port, there are several different styles.

Manzanilla: The lightest type of sherry, made from wine matured in Sanlucar de Barrameda, a little seaside town. Manzanilla is light, dry and tangy; it is very good as an aperitif, when it is best served chilled.

Fino: It's another light, dry sherry (although it's sometimes sweetened). It is also good as an aperitif. Serve chilled, and don't keep the bottle too long: fino and manzanilla don't keep well after they've been opened.

Amontillado: This is fino that has matured to a darker, nuttier colour and flavour. Amontillados are often sweetened to medium-sweet for export, but the best ones are dry.

Oloroso: This sherry has always had a richer, darker colour than fino and amontillado. 'Oloroso' actually means 'fragrant', and even dry olorosos smell sweetly raisiny. Most of the olorosos sold in Britain are sweet; they are a good alternative to port after dinner.

Pale Cream: A third-rate fino which has been sweetened up for export.

Cream: This is a very sweet type of oloroso sherry.

Palo Cortado: This lies somewhere between amontillado and oloroso in flavour. It is still quite a rarity, with a deliciously nutty flavour, and can be dry or slightly sweetened.

British 'Sherry': This is not proper sherry at all but made from imported grape concentrate in Britain, and is usually unpleasant.

Madeira

The fortified wines of Madeira, a semi-tropical, volcanic island 450 miles off the coast of Morocco, used to be famous. Sercial, Verdelho, Bual and Malmsey were the names of the grapes, and of the wines. Plantations of these noble grapes are now very small, and most Madeira is made from another, less distinguished grape, and just sold as dry, medium-dry, medium-sweet and sweet. However, the tangy, baked (part

of the production process involves heating the maturing wine) flavour of Madeira is unique, and certainly worth trying, and, of course, it makes the most wonderful sauces.

Fortified Muscats

The Muscat is a grape that makes beautiful fortified wines. They're lush and syrupy, with flavours of orange, treacle and flowers, and always sweet. Some are little more than grape juice with some alcohol added, while others partly ferment the juice before adding the alcohol. Either way, they make marvellous partners for orange, toffee or chocolate-flavoured desserts, or for just sipping by themselves at the end of a meal.

Above: Charles Metcalfe and Richard Madeley discuss festive wines.

The names to look out for include Muscat de Beaumes-de-Venise and Muscat de Rivesaltes from the south of France, Rutherglen Liqueur Muscat from Australia, Moscatel de Valencia from Spain, and Moscatel de Setubal from Portugal.

SPIRITS AND LIQUEURS

Christmas is the time of year when everybody likes to have a few bottles tucked away for a noggin of something warming. Here's my guide to the mysteries of the spirit world.

WHISKY

Do you enjoy Scotch as a drink to mix with water, or ginger ale or as a drink to sip after dinner? If you're a whisky mixer, then I bet it's a blended whisky, whereas it might be a single malt if you enjoy an after-dinner drink. 'Blended' whisky is made from a mixture of lighter grain whisky and more flavourful malt.

'Malt' whisky is distilled from malted barley in pot stills, which are emptied and then refilled after each distillation. It can have flavours as diverse as tarry rope and heather honey. A 'single malt' is the product of a single one of Scotland's nearly 100 distilleries. The so-called 'deluxe' blends can be delicious and subtle blends of malts and grain, and whether you choose a good blend or a single malt, either is a worthy rival to France's great brandies.

Irish whiskey is mostly distilled in pot stills – three times compared to twice for Scotch. It is often richer and smoother than Scotch, but perhaps without such a wide range of flavours. Canadian whiskey is made from rye and is very light. Bourbon has a sweeter flavour than any others, and is distilled from corn and then filtered through charcoal made from sugar maple wood.

BRANDY

Cognac and Armagnac in the south-west of France, are the undisputed stars of the world of brandy.

Armagnac is a much smaller scale industry than Cognac, and is more earthily rustic in flavour, too, compared with the elegance of Cognac. The finest Cognacs are made from grapes grown in the Grande Champagne and Petite Champagne areas of the region. Both Cognac and Armagnac improve in the barrel up to about fifty years old, but the legal age indications are very confusing.

Cognac and Armagnac both have to be at least two years old (Three Star) before they can be sold, although VO (very old) Armagnac also comes into this youngest category. VSOP (Very Special Old Pale) is the next step up at a minimum four years old, or VO or Réserve in Cognac. Then the two regions diverge, with Armagnac permitting five-year-old brandy in Napoleon, XO, Vieille Réserve, Hors d'Age and Trés Vieille, whereas in Cognac the minimum age for all these is six years. However, all Cognacs and most Armagnacs (single-vintage ones are allowed) are blends of brandies of different ages, so there would undoubtedly be older brandies in the blends.

Other than in France, everywhere wine is made, you will find brandy, too. Best known in Britain are Spanish and Greek brandies. It is also made out of the skins and pips left over after fermentation. In France this is called 'marc', and in Italy 'grappa'.

Fruit brandies, or 'eaux de vie' in France, can be made from raspberries (framboise, himbeergeist), pears (poire Williams/Wilhelmsbirne), plums (mirabelle/quetsch), cherries (kirsch), or almost any fruit or berry. They make delicious drinks after a meal, especially served straight from the freezer. Calvados is the most famous of the brandies made from cider, although there is a good English cider brandy made in Somerset.

LIQUEURS

You can group liqueurs by flavour and style, but they are always sweet.

Fruit liqueurs: Apricot brandy, Cherry brandy, Cointreau (orange), Crème de Cassis (blackcurrant), Curaçao (orange), Grand Marnier (orange), Mandarine Napoleon (mandarin), Sloe gin.

Herb liqueurs: Bénédictine, Chartreuse, Crème de Menthe (mint), Drambuie, Galliano, Glayva, Kummel, Strega.

Aniseed liqueurs: Ouzo, Pernod, Raki, Ricard, Pastis, Sambuca.

Assorted Liqueurs: Advocaat (egg), Amaretto (almond), Archers Peach Schnapps, Baileys Irish Cream (chocolate), Kahlua (coffee), Malibu (coconut), Parfait Amour (violet and lemon), Tia Maria (coffee).

NON-ALCOHOLIC DRINKS

MULLED APPLE JUICE

¹/₂ cinnamon stick
3 cloves
pinch of grated nutmeg
1 litre/1²/₃ pints clear apple juice
1 apple, cored and sliced

1 Make an infusion of the spices by putting the cinnamon stick, cloves and nutmeg in a mugful of boiling water, and then simmer for 15 minutes.
2 Strain off the spices, and pour the spicy liquid into the apple juice. Heat through gently until it is hot enough to serve. Decorate each glass with a slice of apple.
Note: You can vary this recipe by substituting other fruit juices for the apple juice, e.g. pineapple or orange. Decorate the glasses with a slice of the appropriate fruit.
MAKES: approximately 1 litre/1²/₃ pints

DRINKS FOR DRIVERS

Steer clear of alcohol-free wines: there are so many drinks that taste better! Producers seem to have succeeded much more with alcohol-free beers, so I wouldn't mind one or two of those if I were driving. However, a can of beer is rather a drab drink for a celebratory occasion. Better far to get the creativity working and come up with some good combinations using some of the increasingly exotic fruit juices available in cartons at supermarkets.

Fruit juices whizzed up in a food-processor with some fresh fruit, mulled with an infusion of spices, combined with coconut cream, given a lift by tonic water - there are lots of possibilities. Using milk as a base, you can invent quite a few grown-up milkshakes, which are very sophisticated.

CHOCOLATE GUNK

10 heaped teaspoons chocolate hazelnut spread
600ml/1 pint full-cream milk
4 heaped tablespoons 8% fat fromage frais

1 Put the chocolate hazelnut spread and milk in a saucepan and place over medium heat. Stir gently until the chocolate hazelnut spread dissolves.
2 Remove from the heat and allow to cool slightly, and then transfer to a blender and whizz it up with the fromage frais. Drink warm, or chill in the refrigerator before serving cold. If so, stir before serving.
MAKES: approximately 600ml/1 pint

PARTY DRINKS

MULLED WHITE WINE

2 cinnamon sticks
6 cardamom pods, lightly crushed
1/2 teaspoon grated nutmeg
3 tangerines (or mandarins or clementines), sliced
110g/4oz barley sugar sweets
1 bottle inexpensive German white wine

1 Make a spiced 'tea': add the cinnamon, cardamom pods, grated nutmeg and 2 of the sliced tangerines to 500ml/17 fl oz boiling water. Reduce the heat and simmer for 20 minutes. Strain off the spices and fruit, and keep the liquid.
2 Dissolve the barley sugars in 350ml/12 fl oz boiling water. Reduce the heat and stir in the white wine, together with 200ml/7 fl oz of the strained spiced 'tea'. Heat gently without boiling. You can vary the amounts of barley-sugar water and spiced 'tea' to suit your taste. Serve in glasses decorated with the remaining sliced tangerine.
MAKES: approximately 1 litre/1²/3 pints

PUNCH

There is one simple rule when making hot punches or mulled drinks: never let them boil. Alcohol evaporates very quickly, so if you want your drinks to have any when you serve them, heat them for the shortest time possible. If you're mulling wine or cider, and want to get a good, spicy flavour into it (from nutmeg, cloves, cinnamon or whatever), do make an infusion of spices first as the recipes suggest, and only add your wine or cider at the last possible moment. Of course, if you want to go easy on the alcohol, there's nothing better than either a hot punch or mulled drink to give the impression of warmth without booze. If the drink is hot, it warms the drinker, whether it's alcoholic or not, and creates an atmosphere of relaxed conviviality. And you can stop adding brandy, rum or your chosen spirit after the the first or second batch.

Make sure you have cups or glasses that can be held with a hot drink inside them. Wine glasses with stems will do: you can hold them by the stem or the base without burning your fingers on the bowl. And it's much easier to pour from a small jug than from a saucepan or a ladle. Just dip the jug into the saucepan when you need to refill it. Happy mulling!

HOT TODDY

For each serving:
50ml/2 fl oz dark rum (or brandy or whisky)
juice of 1/4 lemon
1 heaped teaspoon unrefined Demerara sugar
115ml/4 fl oz boiling water

You can make a hot toddy with rum, whisky or brandy, depending on which spirit you prefer. Mix the spirit with the lemon juice and sugar, and then add the boiling water, stirring to dissolve the sugar. This makes a good, warming drink on a cold day.
SERVES: 1

MULLED RED WINE

1/2 cinnamon stick
3 cloves
pinch of grated nutmeg
7.5cm/3-inch piece thinly pared lemon rind
1 bottle inexpensive full-bodied red wine
4 tablespoons unrefined Demerara sugar
1 orange, thinly sliced, to decorate

1 Add the cinnamon stick, cloves, nutmeg and lemon rind to a mugful of boiling water. Reduce the heat and simmer

gently for 15 minutes. Strain and keep the spiced liquid.

2 Pour the red wine into a large saucepan and add the spiced liquid and sugar. Heat through gently, but do not allow it to boil. Test to see whether the wine is sweet enough, and add a little more sugar if necessary. Serve in glasses decorated with slices of orange.

MAKES: approximately 1 litre/1²/₃ pints

MULLED CIDER

¹/₂ cinnamon stick
3 cloves
pinch of grated nutmeg
1 litre/1²/₃ pints dry cider
2-3 tablespoons unrefined light brown sugar
50ml/2 fl oz dark rum
sliced apple, to decorate

1 Add the cinnamon stick, cloves and nutmeg to a mugful of boiling water. Reduce the heat and simmer gently for 15 minutes. Strain off the spices and keep the liquid.

2 Add this infused liquid to the cider and sweeten with sugar. Heat gently, without boiling, in a saucepan. Just before serving, stir in the rum. Serve in glasses decorated with slices of apple.

MAKES: approximately 1.2 litres/2 pints

CHAMPAGNE CUP

1 orange, thinly sliced
1 lemon, thinly sliced
1 apple, cored and thinly sliced
110ml/ 4 fl oz brandy
1 bottle chilled sparkling wine, e.g. Australian, Italian,
Spanish, New Zealand or South African
500ml/17 fl oz chilled lemonade

1 Put the sliced orange, lemon and apple in a bowl and add the brandy. Cover with cling film and leave to soak overnight in the refrigerator.

2 The following day, when you are ready to serve the Champagne Cup, transfer the fruit and brandy to a large

glass jug or punch bowl, and add the sparkling wine and chilled lemonade. If you like a more alcoholic drink, you can add more brandy or some orange liqueur, such as Cointreau, Curaçao or Grand Marnier. If you prefer it to be less alcoholic, just add more lemonade until you reach the desired balance and flavour.

MAKES: approximately 1.6 litres/2³/₄ pints

PART FIVE

FESTIVE FOOD

In this chapter, you will find all your favourite
Christmas recipes plus some more unusual
ideas for entertaining and using up leftovers.
There are menus for Christmas Eve and Boxing
Day family meals, snacks for hungry carol
singers and an alternative vegetarian Christmas
dinner. If you follow our experts' advice, you
will be so well organised that you can sit down
and put your feet up after serving the turkey.

CHRISTMAS EVE FAMILY SUPPER

SUSAN BROOKES

MENU

SALMON MOUSSE GARLAND

HONEY GLAZED HAM (SEE PAGE 32)

YORKSHIRE SAUCE (SEE PAGE 32)

APRICOT AND ALMOND STUFFING

BAKED POTATOES AND SALAD

CHOCOLATE BLISS

SALMON MOUSSE GARLAND

560g/1¹/₄lb fresh salmon
juice of ¹/₂ lemon
salt and pepper
15g/¹/₂oz powdered gelatine (1 sachet)
75ml/3 fl oz hot water
150ml/¹/₄ pint mayonnaise
150ml/¹/₄ pint thick natural yogurt
1 teaspoon mustard
1-2 teaspoons paprika
300ml/¹/₂ pint double cream
5 slices smoked salmon

1 Put a little crumpled foil in the base of a large saucepan and place the salmon on top. Cover with cold water and add the lemon juice and seasoning. Bring slowly up to a simmer, and then simmer gently for 1 minute. Remove

Left: Salmon Mousse Garland

from the heat, cover the pan and leave the fish to cool in the poaching liquid. This way, the salmon will be cooked through and really moist. Skin, bone and flake the cool salmon, and set aside.

2 Sprinkle the gelatine on to the hot water and leave for 5 minutes to dissolve. Warm the water gently and stir thoroughly if it has not dissolved after this time, but do not boil.

3 Mix the mayonnaise and yogurt together, and add the gelatine liquid, mustard and paprika, and mix well. Stir in the flaked salmon and season to taste with a little salt and ground black pepper.

4 Whip the cream until it just holds its shape, and then fold into the salmon mixture. Line a 25cm/10-inch ring mould with cling film, and arrange the slices of smoked salmon at regular intervals around the mould, leaving gaps between each slice and overlapping the edges.

5 Pour the salmon mixture into the mould and fold any spare edges of smoked salmon over the top. Refrigerate for several hours until set, preferably overnight. To serve, turn the mould out upside-down on to a plate, and serve garnished with herbs, watercress or lettuce leaves arranged around the sides of the plate to resemble a Christmas garland or piled into the centre of the Salmon Mousse Garland.

SERVES: 8

APRICOT AND ALMOND STUFFING

225g/8oz dried apricots
225g/8oz brown bread, crusts removed
50g/2oz butter
1 onion, finely chopped
115g/4oz flaked almonds, toasted
2 teaspoons dried mixed herbs
salt and pepper
2 eggs, beaten

1 Put the apricots and bread in a food processor, with the metal blade fitted. Process until the apricots are well chopped and the bread is crumbed.

2 Melt the butter in a saucepan and add the onion. Cook gently in the butter until it softens, about 5-10 minutes. Transfer to a bowl and add the breadcrumb mixture and almonds. Stir gently until thoroughly combined.

3 Mix in the herbs and seasoning with a fork and then stir in the beaten eggs. Mix well until the mixture lightly binds together, and place in a greased shallow, ovenproof dish. Smooth the top, and then bake in a preheated oven at 200°C/400°F/Gas Mark 6 for about 15 minutes, until crisp and slightly browned on top. Alternatively, you can roll the mixture into balls before baking.

SERVES: 8

CHOCOLATE BLISS

4 x 100g/3¹/₂oz bars plain chocolate
4 tablespoons Cointreau or brandy
5 tablespoons golden syrup
450ml/³/₄ pint double cream
icing sugar, for dusting

1 Break the chocolate into pieces and place in a bowl over a saucepan of barely simmering water. Add the Cointreau and syrup and leave until melted and smooth, stirring occasionally. Remove from the heat and pour into another cold bowl to cool down quickly.

2 Leave to cool for 10 minutes, stirring from time to time. Don't be tempted to speed this up by placing the chocolate mixture in the refrigerator – it will cool too much and will be too stiff to mix.

3 Whisk the cream until it is thick and holds its shape. Mix 1 spoonful of cream into the chocolate mixture to 'slacken' it. Gently fold in the remaining cream, and pour into 8 small serving glasses. If you want to make the pudding more than a day ahead of serving, make sure that the glasses are freezer-proof. Leave to chill in the refrigerator overnight (or freeze until required).

4 To serve the Chocolate Bliss, dust lightly with sifted icing sugar immediately before serving. This creates an attractive frosted effect and is less rich and heavy than decorating with cream.

SERVES: 8

CHRISTMAS EVE DINNER

BRIAN TURNER

MENU

RED PEPPER AND TOMATO BAVAROIS

AGNEAU GASCONNADE

CARAMELIZED POTATOES (SEE PAGE 107)

PAN-FRIED SPINACH

PRUNE TART WITH ALMONDS

RED PEPPER AND TOMATO BAVAROIS

25g/1oz shallots, chopped
25g/1oz butter
2 tomatoes, skinned, seeded and chopped
2 red peppers, seeded and chopped
3 leaves gelatine, or 1 sachet
2 tablespoons white wine vinegar
pinch each of cayenne and paprika
300ml/^{1}/$_2$ pint whipped cream

For the dressing:
2 tomatoes, skinned, seeded and chopped
175g/6oz peeled, cooked prawns
3 tablespoons olive oil
1 tablespoon white wine vinegar
salt and freshly ground black pepper
1 tablespoon chopped chives

1 Cook the shallots gently in butter, until softened. Add the tomatoes and peppers, and cook gently until soft.

Purée the vegetable mixture in a food processor.
2 Soften the gelatine in cold water. Meanwhile, boil the vinegar in a small pan until reduced by half. Squeeze out the excess water from the gelatine and melt in the vinegar. Add the cayenne and paprika, and stir well.
3 Mix the gelatine liquid into the puréed vegetables and stir well. Set aside to cool, and then mix in the whipped cream. Before the mixture sets, pour into 6 individual moulds which have been lined with cling film. Put in the refrigerator until set.
4 Just before serving, mix all the dressing ingredients together. Turn out the moulds on to 6 serving plates and spoon the dressing over the top.
SERVES: 6

AGNEAU GASCONNADE

1 × 2.2kg/5lb leg of mutton
10 anchovy fillets, drained
6 garlic cloves, peeled
pinch of salt
1 bunch of parsley, finely chopped
pan-fried spinach, to serve

1 Ask the butcher to remove the aitch bone and thigh bone from the mutton to leave a cavity inside. Pound the anchovy fillets with the garlic and salt in a mortar, until you have a thick paste. Mix in the chopped parsley, and use this mixture to stuff the boned-out mutton. Tie with string to enclose the filling securely.
2 Place the mutton on a rack in a roasting pan, and roast in a preheated oven at 200°C/400°F/Gas Mark 6. After 10 minutes, reduce the oven temperature to 180°C/350°F/Gas Mark 4 and cook for a further 1^1/$_4$ hours.
3 Remove the string from the cooked mutton, and serve on a bed of pan-fried spinach.
SERVES: 6

PRUNE TART WITH ALMONDS

175g/6oz sweet pastry
1 egg, beaten
24 prunes, stoned
3-4 tablespoons Armagnac
75g/3oz ground almonds
3 eggs
115g/4oz sugar
grated zest of 1 orange

1 Line a 22cm/9-inch flan case with the pastry. Fill with greaseproof paper and baking beans, and then bake 'blind' in a preheated oven at 200°C/400°F/Gas Mark 6 for 15 minutes. Remove the paper and beans and brush the inside of the pastry case with beaten egg. Return to the oven for 5 minutes to dry out, and then leave to cool.

2 Meanwhile, soak the prunes in the Armagnac for 15 minutes. Drain the prunes and arrange in the pastry case. Mix together the ground almonds, eggs, sugar and orange zest, and pour over the prunes.

3 Bake the tart in a preheated oven at 200°C/400°F/Gas Mark 6 for 25 minutes, until the filling has set. Serve warm with cream or crème fraîche.

SERVES: 6

Below: Prune Tart with Almonds

CHRISTMAS EVE SNACKS FOR CAROL SINGERS

SUSAN BROOKES

CRISPY BAKED SKINS

These make a delicious late-night snack for Christmas Eve, particularly if you have been to Midnight Mass and are feeling a bit peckish. You can bake the potatoes in advance and finish them off just before serving.

4 large baking potatoes
10 rashers unsmoked streaky bacon, rind removed
115g/4oz grated Cheddar or crumbled Stilton cheese
salt and freshly ground black pepper

1 Scrub the potatoes well and pat dry. Bake them in a preheated oven at 180°C/350°F/Gas Mark 4 for 1¹/4 hours, or until soft when squeezed gently.

2 Grill the bacon rashers until crisp and then crumble into small pieces. Mix two-thirds of the bacon with the cheese and season with a little salt and pepper.
3 Cut each potato in half and scoop out most of the potato flesh, leaving only a thin layer next to the skin. Cut each potato skin in half again. Divide the cheese and bacon mixture and scooped-out potato between the potato 'boats'. Sprinkle with the remaining bacon pieces and place under a preheated grill for 5 minutes, until crisp and sizzling. Serve with soured cream or a dip (see page 122).
SERVES: 4

A SAVOURY QUARTET OF MUFFINS

When we used to go carol singing in our village, we were given hot mince pies and mulled wine to fortify us against the cold. However, if you don't have a sweet tooth, or you want to offer something savoury as well, you could try making these little muffins. They can be baked ahead and then frozen until required. They are small enough to defrost and warm up quickly in a hot oven. To make a dozen muffins of each flavour, you should prepare the flavourings first.

CHEESE AND CHIVE FLAVOURING

Mix 75g/3oz grated strong Cheddar cheese with 1 tablespoon freeze-dried chives, or 2 tablespoons chopped chives.

OLIVE AND TOMATO FLAVOURING

Mix 50g/2oz quartered, stoned black olives with 50g/2oz diced sun-dried tomatoes.

WALNUT AND PARMESAN FLAVOURING

Mix 50g/2oz chopped walnuts with 2 tablespoons grated Parmesan cheese.

ONION BHAJI FLAVOURING

Mix 2 teaspoons curry paste with ½ onion, which has been finely chopped.

For the muffin mixture:
2 teaspoons salt
2 tablespoons baking powder
560g/1¼ lb plain flour
115g/4oz butter
2 eggs
450ml/ ¾ pint milk

1 Sift the salt, baking powder and flour into a large bowl. Melt the butter in a small pan over gentle heat. Whisk the eggs and milk together, and then whisk in the melted butter.
2 Fold the egg mixture into the flour and divide the mixture into 4 portions. Carefully divide the prepared flavours between the different portions, one for each, and fold in gently. Use 2 teaspoons to fill well-greased muffin tins with the muffin mixtures. There should be enough mixture to make 48 muffins.
3 Bake in batches in a preheated oven at 200°C/400°F/Gas Mark 6 for 20 minutes, until well risen and golden brown. Cool in the tin for a few minutes before turning out onto a cooling rack. The muffins are best eaten hot. You can make them in advance and warm them when required.
MAKES: 48 muffins

Below: A Savoury Quartet of Muffins

CHRISTMAS DAY BRUNCH

BRIAN TURNER

MENU

MINI CROQUE MONSIEURS

SCRAMBLED EGGS WITH SMOKED HADDOCK

SPICY TOMATO SAUSAGE PATTIES

BLOODY MARYS

In many households, Christmas dinner is served late – in the afternoon or early evening – so what better way to start the day than with a festive brunch? It is not a breakfast that is every child's dream, but most adults wolf it down, especially if they are feeling a bit delicate after over-indulging themselves the night before!

MINI CROQUE MONSIEURS

8 slices white bread
2 tablespoons horseradish cream
115g/4oz ham (8 slices)
115g/4oz Emmenthal or Gruyère cheese, cut into 8 slices
2 eggs
50ml/2 fl oz cream
salt and freshly ground black pepper
olive oil for shallow-frying

1 Using a scone cutter, or tumbler, cut 16 rounds, 5cm/ 2 inches in diameter, out of the bread slices. Spread 8 of the rounds with horseradish cream and top with a piece of ham and then a slice of cheese. Cover with the remaining bread rounds to make sandwiches.
2 Beat the eggs and cream together, and season well with salt and pepper. Dip the sandwiches in the egg mixture.
3 Heat the oil in a frying pan and add the sandwiches, a few at a time. Shallow-fry gently, turning once, until golden brown on both sides. Remove from the pan and drain on absorbent kitchen paper to soak up any excess fat. Fry the remaining sandwiches and serve immediately.
SERVES: 4

SCRAMBLED EGGS WITH SMOKED HADDOCK

225g/8oz smoked haddock fillet, thinly sliced
juice of 1 lime
salt and freshly ground black pepper
splash of olive oil
6 eggs
25g/1oz butter, melted
50ml/2 fl oz single cream or yogurt
salad leaves, to garnish
French dressing, to serve

1 Place the haddock slices on a plate. Squeeze the lime juice over the top and sprinkle with salt, pepper and olive oil. Leave to marinate for about 20 minutes.
2 Beat the eggs and mix in the melted butter. Add the cream or yogurt and season with salt and pepper. Pour into a saucepan and stir constantly with a wooden spoon over low heat, until the eggs start to scramble.
3 Line 4 small moulds with cling film and then line the moulds with the haddock fillets, leaving some overhanging the edges. Fill the moulds with the scrambled eggs and fold the haddock fillets over the top to seal in the egg mixture.
4 Turn out the moulds on to a plate, and serve warm, garnished with salad leaves. Pour a little French dressing over the top.
SERVES: 4

SPICY TOMATO SAUSAGE PATTIES

225g/8oz sausagemeat
50ml/2 fl oz tomato ketchup
dash of Tabasco sauce
2 tablespoons chopped fresh parsley
1 egg, beaten
olive oil for shallow-frying

1 Mix together all the ingredients except the olive oil in a bowl. When it binds together, hand-roll the mixture into small, walnut-sized balls, and tap them flat.
2 Shallow-fry the balls in hot olive oil until they are golden brown on both sides. Drain and serve immediately.
SERVES: 4

Below: Scrambled Eggs with Smoked Haddock (right) and mini Croque Monsieur (left).

BLOODY MARY

1 double measure Absolut vodka
splash of Worcestershire sauce
splash of lime juice
splash of chilli juice
celery salt, to season
crushed ice
110ml/4 fl oz tomato juice
1 fresh oyster and juice (optional)
1 lemon slice, to decorate

1 Mix the vodka. Worcestershire sauce, lime juice and chilli juice. Season to taste with celery salt and mix with crushed ice.
2 Transfer to a glass and top up with tomato juice. Add the oyster and juice (if using) and serve with a slice of lemon.
SERVES: 1

CHRISTMAS DAY LUNCH STARTERS

SALMON PATTIE CAKES

BRIAN TURNER

115g/4oz button mushrooms, diced
40g/1¹/₂oz butter
squeeze of lemon juice
20g/³/₄oz flour
150ml/¹/₄ pint milk
1 egg yolk
salt and freshly ground black pepper
pinch of freshly grated nutmeg
225g/8oz cooked salmon, skinned and boned
50g/2oz fresh breadcrumbs
1 egg, beaten
oil for shallow-frying
lemon wedges, to serve

1 Sauté the mushrooms gently in 15g/¹/₂oz of the butter, until cooked and golden. Remove from the pan, squeeze the lemon juice over them and set aside.

2 Melt the remaining butter in a clean saucepan and stir in the flour. Cook for 2-3 minutes over gentle heat without colouring. Add the milk gradually, stirring all the time, until the sauce is thick and smooth. Remove from the heat and beat in the egg yolk.

3 Add the mushrooms in their cooking juices to the white sauce. Stir over low heat until thickened. Season to taste with salt, pepper and nutmeg. Flake the salmon and stir gently into the sauce. Remove from the heat and transfer to a bowl. Cover and cool a little, and then place in the refrigerator until cold and solid.

4 Lightly toast the breadcrumbs. Remove the cold sauce from the refrigerator and, with well-floured hands, mould into 8 balls of equal size. Flatten with your hands and then dip each pattie into beaten egg and then the toasted breadcrumbs.

5 Shallow-fry in hot oil until the patties are golden brown and crisp on both sides. Serve hot with lemon wedges.
SERVES: 4

SMOKED HADDOCK PUFFS

BRIAN TURNER

This first course looks very impressive but it is easy to make. It can be assembled in advance if you store the pastry puffs in an airtight container, and keep the haddock and tomato sauces separately in the refrigerator. You can then reheat everything on the day and put the dish together.

1 × 250g/9oz packet frozen puff pastry, thawed
1 egg, beaten
1 teaspoon sesame seeds
50g/2oz butter
4 tomatoes, skinned and quartered
1 garlic clove, crushed
salt and freshly ground black pepper
225g/8oz smoked haddock fillet, skinned and diced
50g/2oz cucumber, diced
1 tablespoon balsamic vinegar
2-3 tablespoons thick Greek yogurt
sprigs of fresh dill, to garnish

1 Roll out the pastry on a lightly floured surface, until it is about 1mm/¹/₁₆-inch thick. Stamp out 12 circles, 6cm/ 2¹/₂ inches in diameter, with a glass tumbler. Place them on a baking sheet and prick lightly with a fork.

2 Brush the pastry circles with beaten egg and sprinkle 4 of the circles with sesame seeds. Bake in a preheated oven at 220°C/425°F/Gas Mark 7 for 8-10 minutes, or until risen and golden brown. Cool on a wire rack.

3 Meanwhile, melt half of the butter in a small saucepan and add the tomatoes and garlic. Cook gently for about 10 minutes, or until the sauce thickens. Season to taste with salt and pepper and then set aside.

4 In another pan, melt the remaining butter and add the haddock and cucumber. Cook, stirring gently, until the haddock is just cooked. Transfer to a bowl and stir in the vinegar and enough yogurt to bind the mixture together.

Above: Smoked Haddock Puffs

5 Divide the tomato sauce between 4 serving plates. Place a plain pastry circle on each plate and spoon some of the haddock mixture on top. Cover with another plain pastry circle and top with the remaining haddock mixture. Cover with the sesame pastry circles and serve with fresh dill.
SERVES: 4

MELON WITH STILTON AND WATERCRESS SAUCE

SUSAN BROOKES

If you want to serve a starter before the roast turkey or goose, then it has to be something light. This recipe is ideal as it is very refreshing and quick and easy to prepare. You can make it more colourful by using different varieties of melons.

1 bunch of watercress
115g/4oz Stilton cheese, rind removed
squeeze of lemon juice
150ml/¹/4 pint natural yogurt
1 large or 3 small melons

1 Put the watercress and Stilton cheese in the food processor, with the metal blade fitted. Process until the watercress is well chopped. Add the lemon juice and yogurt and blend together. Pour this sauce into a bowl, cover and chill in the refrigerator until required. It will thicken as it chills.
2 Peel the melon(s) and remove the seeds. Cut the flesh into thick slices and serve with the chilled sauce.
SERVES: 6

CHRISTMAS DAY

SUSAN BROOKES

THE TURKEY

When choosing a turkey, only you can decide whether a fresh one is worth the extra money in terms of flavour. Personally, I think it is, but there is no doubt that there are some very cheap frozen birds you can buy. Always take care when handling and cooking turkeys, especially if frozen. Here are some guidelines to help you.

1 Make sure you follow the instructions on the label of a frozen bird, especially as regards thawing times, which are often a lot longer than you might think.

2 A fresh bird, too, should be taken out of the refrigerator several hours before cooking so that it starts to cook as soon as it goes into the oven. If you are planning an early lunch, do this before you go to bed on Christmas Eve; if you are eating later in the day, take the turkey out first thing in the morning.

3 Always remember to take the giblets out! You wouldn't be the first person to cook a turkey containing a polythene bag filled with bits of innards! Do check.

STUFFING THE TURKEY

I only ever stuff the neck end, pushing the chosen stuffing well up under the breast skin, but not packing it too tightly in case it bursts the skin – stuffing tends to expand slightly during cooking. The remaining stuffing can be cooked separately in a greased ovenproof dish for 30 minutes in a moderate to hot oven, and will be crisp and golden brown on top if it is cooked uncovered.

Fill the body cavity of the turkey with a quartered onion, a handful of herbs, such as thyme or parsley, and a knob of butter. Fold the neck flap of skin under the bird to hold in the stuffing, and then tie the legs together with some string, taking it around the 'parson's nose' to make a neat shape. Sometimes you can push the leg ends through a slit that the butcher has made for this purpose.

READY FOR THE OVEN

Again, if you are eating early, prepare the turkey on Christmas Eve so that all you have to do on the day is to put it in the oven. Make a large cross shape with two pieces of wide foil, and put a big roasting pan under the middle of the cross. Place the turkey in the centre, and smear about

115g/4oz butter over the surface of the skin. Put more butter towards the top than the bottom, as it will trickle down as it melts. Season with salt and freshly ground black pepper, and then bring the opposite sides of the foil up into the middle to make a tent. Fold the edges of the foil together to seal it, but do not pull them tightly around the turkey – there should be some space inside the foil.

When you have decided on the time at which you want to sit down and eat, add 30 minutes standing time on to the time for cooking in the oven – more for a large bird. The turkey will carve more easily, and be more succulent, if given this resting time. A turkey is large enough to stay hot for some time in a reasonably warm kitchen, which I'm sure your kitchen will be by that time!

CALCULATING COOKING TIMES

A family of eight or ten people should have plenty to eat with a 5.5-6.5kg/12-14lb oven-ready turkey. I recommend cooking at a high temperature to begin with, then slower for the main part of the cooking time, and a last high period to brown the breast. The cooking chart (above right) is a guide, but bear in mind that ovens vary and you should know if yours tends to cook more quickly, especially if it is a fan-assisted one.

During the last part of the cooking, fold back the foil to uncover the top of the turkey and baste frequently with the cooking juices. You can test to see whether the turkey is cooked by sticking a skewer into the fleshiest part of the thigh. If the turkey is ready, the juices will run clear; otherwise put it back in the oven for a little while longer.

GRAVY

Brace yourself! Those nasty-looking squidgy bits inside the body cavity of the turkey are called giblets and you are in for a treat if you don't throw them away. Remove them from the turkey as soon as you bring it home. Tip them into a saucepan and cover with cold water. Bring to the boil and then simmer for 1 hour. This will make a delicious

COOKING CHART

Size of bird	start at 220°C/425°F/ Gas Mark 7	turn down to 170°C/325°F/ Gas Mark 3	finish at 200°C/400°F/ Gas Mark 6
Small 3.5-5kg/ 8-11lb	30 minutes	3 hours	30 minutes
Total cooking time: 4 hours. Stand for 30 minutes.			
Medium 5.5-6.5kg/ 12-14lb	45 minutes	3½ hours	45 minutes
Total cooking time: 5 hours. Stand for 35 minutes.			
Large 6.75-9kg/ 15-20lb	1 hour	4½ hours	45 minutes
Total cooking time: 6¼ hours. Stand for 40 minutes.			

stock which you can use to make the gravy. Cool and then pour into a container, cover and refrigerate until required. The boiled turkey giblets can be cooled and then given to the cat for a Christmas treat.

To make the gravy: remove the cooked turkey from the roasting pan, together with any pieces of foil sticking to the base of the pan. Drain off most of the fat into a basin and, when cool, store in the refrigerator for cooking future roasts. Leave a little fat in the pan and place over low heat. Work in 2 tablespoons plain flour with some salt, pepper and a little gravy browning, if wished. Stir well to scrape up the sticky bits and residue on the base of the pan. Heat the reserved giblet stock and gradually add to the pan, stirring all the time.

Bring to the boil and let the gravy bubble for a while until it reduces and thickens a little. This will also improve and concentrate the flavour. If the gravy is too thick, you can add a little of the hot vegetable water, a glass of red wine, port or Marsala. Check the seasoning, pour into a gravy boat and serve.

STUFFINGS AND SAUCES

SUSAN BROOKES

APPLE AND APRICOT STUFFING

225g/8oz chopped onion
50g/2oz butter
1 cooking apple, peeled, cored and grated
2 tablespoons lemon juice
75g/3oz no-soak dried apricots
115g/4oz coarse oatmeal, toasted
3 tablespoons chopped fresh sage (or 1 teaspoon dried)
225g/8oz fresh brown breadcrumbs
1 egg (size 3), beaten
salt and pepper

1 Fry the onion in the butter in a frying pan, until soft and golden. Stir in the apple and lemon juice, and then spoon into a large mixing bowl.
2 Snip the apricots into small pieces and add to the bowl. Mix in the oatmeal, sage, breadcrumbs, beaten egg and seasoning, stirring until thoroughly mixed. Use as a stuffing for turkey or chicken.
SERVES: 6

LIGHT CHESTNUT STUFFING

40g/1¹/₂oz butter
1 onion, finely chopped
115g/4oz mushrooms, finely chopped
1 × 225g/8oz can of peeled whole chestnuts
75g/3oz fresh brown breadcrumbs
1 tablespoon chopped fresh parsley
salt and pepper
1 egg (size 3), beaten

1 Melt the butter in a saucepan, add the onion and fry gently until golden and softened. Do not allow the onion to brown. Add the mushrooms and fry for 1 minute.
2 Drain the chestnuts and chop them roughly. Place in a large bowl with the fried onion and mushroom mixture, breadcrumbs, parsley and seasoning. Mix well and then pour in the beaten egg. Bind together with a fork.
3 Use the stuffing to stuff the neck end of the turkey, or cook it separately in an ovenproof dish in a preheated oven at 200°C/400°F/Gas Mark 6 for 15 minutes, until crisp.
SERVES: 6-8

THYME AND TARRAGON STUFFING

2 onions, finely chopped
1 garlic clove, crushed
2.5cm/1-inch piece fresh root ginger, peeled and chopped
1 tablespoon oil
15g/¹/₂oz butter
1 stick celery, chopped
225g/8oz good-quality sausagemeat
115g/4oz no-soak dried apricots, chopped
50g/2oz fresh breadcrumbs
grated zest of 1 lemon
1 tablespoon each of chopped parsley, tarragon and thyme
1 egg (size 3), beaten
salt and pepper, to taste

1 Fry the onions, garlic and ginger in the oil and butter, until soft and golden. Add the celery and cook gently for 2-3 minutes. Remove from the heat and leave to cool.
2 Mix together the sausagemeat, apricots, breadcrumbs, lemon zest and herbs. Add the cooked onion mixture, beaten egg and seasoning, and stir well. Use for stuffing the turkey.
SERVES: 8-10

SAGE AND SAUSAGE STUFFING

50g/2oz unsalted butter
2 onions, chopped
2 Bramley apples, peeled, cored and chopped
2 teaspoons dried sage
grated zest and juice of 1 lemon
675g/1¹/₂lb good-quality sausagemeat
50g/2oz breadcrumbs
salt and freshly ground black pepper

1 Melt the butter in a frying pan and add the onions and apples. Cook over low heat until softened, and then stir in the sage, lemon zest and juice. Set aside to cool.
2 Break up the sausagemeat in a large bowl and add the breadcrumbs. Mix well and then stir in the apple, sage and onion mixture. Season with salt and pepper. Use as a stuffing for the turkey or place in a greased ovenproof dish and cook with the roast.
SERVES: 8-10

TURKEY STUFFING

2 onions, finely chopped
2 tablespoons unsalted butter
450g/1lb prunes, soaked, stoned and chopped
450g/1lb dried apricots, soaked, stoned and chopped
115g/4oz seedless raisins
4 apples, peeled, cored and chopped
115g/4oz walnuts, roughly chopped
salt and freshly ground black pepper
2 teaspoons ground cinnamon

1 Sauté the onions in the butter until soft and golden. Add the prunes, apricots, raisins, apples and walnuts, and cook gently until the fruit plumps up.
2 Remove from the heat and season to taste with salt and pepper. Stir in the cinnamon and allow to cool before using to stuff the turkey.
SERVES: 8

BREAD SAUCE

BRIAN TURNER

300ml/¹/₂ pint milk
1 onion, studded with 1 clove
1 bay leaf
4 peppercorns
pinch of grated nutmeg
75g/3oz fresh white breadcrumbs
25g/1oz butter
splash of double cream
salt and freshly ground black pepper

1 Put the milk in a small saucepan and add the clove-studded onion, bay leaf, peppercorns and nutmeg. Bring to the boil, then reduce the heat and simmer very gently for 20 minutes, until the onion is cooked and tender.
2 Remove from the heat and stir in the breadcrumbs. Heat through gently and mix in the butter and cream. Season to taste with salt and pepper. Serve hot with the roast turkey. It also goes well with roast chicken or pheasant.
MAKES: 300ml/¹/₂ pint sauce

Tip: Don't forget to serve some cranberry sauce, too. This is a delicious fruity accompaniment to turkey, and you will find a recipe for traditional Cranberry Orange Sauce on page 46.

BASTING THE TURKEY

You can make a delicious spiced butter for basting the turkey as it cooks. Just add 1 teaspoon each of ground allspice and cinnamon to 115g/4oz softened butter. Mix well and spread over the turkey before wrapping in foil and placing in the oven.

VEGETABLES AND TRIMMINGS

ROAST POTATOES

SUSAN BROOKES

If you parboil the potatoes before roasting them, they will absorb more fat and have a crisper finish. Alternatively, you can peel the potatoes and cut them into pieces. Leave them in salted water for 10 minutes, and then drain well before roasting them.

Whichever method you use, it is very important to get the roasting pan containing the fat really hot before you add the potatoes. Baste them well in the hot fat before

Below: Roast Turkey, Stuffing Balls and Roast Potatoes

roasting, and again after 10 minutes in the oven. They will take about 1 hour to cook and get really crisp and brown in a hot oven, and you should baste them once or twice while they are cooking.

I roast potatoes in a mixture of 2 tablespoons of hot vegetable oil and 1 tablespoon of butter. This gives them a delicious flavour, but many people swear by 75g/3oz lard. If you are worried about getting the potatoes crisp in an oven that seems full up with turkey, make sure that you calculate your cooking times so that the turkey comes out of the oven about 30 minutes before you want to sit down and eat. This will not only give the turkey enough time to stand before carving but it will also give you enough space in the oven to finish off the potatoes.

RED CABBAGE WITH CRANBERRIES

SUSAN BROOKES

25g/1oz butter
1 onion, thinly sliced
675g/1¹/₂lb red cabbage, thinly sliced
2 tablespoons soft brown sugar
2 tablespoons red wine vinegar
150ml/¹/₄ pint red wine
225g/8oz cranberries, fresh or frozen
salt and pepper

1 Melt the butter in a large saucepan and cook the onion until softened but not brown. Add the red cabbage and stir well. Cook gently for 5 minutes and then add the sugar, red wine vinegar and red wine.
2 Bring to the boil, then reduce the heat and cover the pan. Cook gently for about 1 hour, until the cabbage is soft and well reduced. Stir in the cranberries and cook for a further 15-20 minutes. They will 'pop' and soften. If the cabbage mixture is getting too dry, add a little extra red wine. Season to taste with salt and pepper before serving. You can make this a day in advance and store overnight in the refrigerator. The flavour improves on keeping.
SERVES: 8-10

NUTTY SPROUTS

SUSAN BROOKES

50g/2oz chopped hazelnuts, toasted
50g/2oz unsalted butter, softened
salt and freshly ground black pepper
2 garlic cloves, crushed
1kg/2lb Brussels sprouts

1 Mix the hazelnuts with the butter, seasoning and crushed garlic until well blended.
2 Cook the sprouts in boiling salted water until they are just tender but retain a little 'bite'. Drain and toss the sprouts in the nutty butter. Serve immediately.
SERVES: 8-10

CARAMELIZED POTATOES

BRIAN TURNER

40 small new potatoes, unpeeled
50g/2oz caster sugar
50g/2oz unsalted butter, melted

1 Cook the potatoes in salted boiling water for 15-20 minutes, until just tender. Drain and cool slightly before peeling off the skins.
2 Melt the sugar in a heavy frying pan over very low heat. Cook slowly for 3-5 minutes, until the sugar turns to a light brown caramel. Stir constantly with a wooden spoon, watching the sugar closely to ensure that it does not become too dark.
3 Stir in the melted butter and add as many potatoes as possible without crowding the pan. Shake the pan gently to roll the potatoes in the caramel and coat them on all sides. Remove to a heated serving dish, and repeat until all the potatoes are coated.
SERVES: 8-10

Tip: For low-fat Christmas recipes, turn to Rosemary Conley's suggestions for Roast Turkey and Low-Calorie Christmas Pudding on pages 129-130.

VEGETARIAN CHRISTMAS DAY

SUSAN BROOKES

RED PEPPER AND BROCCOLI GOUGERES

For the choux pastry:
50g/2oz butter, diced
150ml/¹/₄ pint water
65g/2 ¹/₂oz strong plain flour
2 eggs (size 3), lightly beaten
50g/2oz vegetarian Cheddar cheese, grated

For the sauce:
1 large red pepper, seeded and diced
450g/1lb broccoli florets
25g/1oz butter
25g/1oz plain flour
300ml/¹/₂ pint milk
2 tablespoons chopped fresh parsley
salt and pepper
1 heaped teaspoon whole-grain mustard

1 Make the sauce first: blanch the red pepper and broccoli in boiling water for 3-5 minutes. Drain, refresh in cold water and then drain well again.

2 Melt the butter in a saucepan and stir in the flour. Cook gently for 2 minutes without browning, stirring all the time. Remove from the heat and stir in the milk, a little at a time, until the sauce is smooth and free from lumps.

3 Return to the heat and bring to the boil, stirring frequently. Stir in the parsley and season to taste. Fold in the red pepper, broccoli and mustard. Keep the sauce warm while you make the choux pastry.

4 To make the pastry, put the butter and water in a saucepan and heat gently until the fat melts. Bring to a full rolling boil, then remove from the heat and tip in the flour immediately. Beat vigorously until the mixture forms a ball of dough. Allow to cool for 5 minutes.

5 Gradually beat in the eggs, a little at a time, until well blended. The mixture should be glossy and of a piping consistency. Place in a piping bag fitted with a wide nozzle and pipe around 4 well-greased scallop-shaped ovenproof dishes. Sprinkle with grated cheese and bake in a preheated oven at 200°C/400°F/Gas Mark 6 for 20-25 minutes.

6 Reheat the sauce and divide between the dishes. Pop under a hot grill for 2-3 minutes to brown. Serve immediately.
SERVES: 4

FILO CRACKERS

115g/4oz butter
16 sheets of filo pastry, 20 × 10cm/8 × 4 inches
melted butter for brushing

For the filling:
20g/³/₄oz packet of dried mushrooms
150ml/¹/₄ pint hot water
50g/2oz butter
1 tablespoon olive oil
350g/12oz parsnips, diced
4cm/1¹/₂-inch piece of fresh root ginger, peeled and finely chopped
4 garlic cloves, crushed
110g/4oz dried apricots, soaked and chopped
1 × 425g/15oz can of whole peeled chestnuts
50g/2oz walnuts, roughly chopped
salt and freshly ground black pepper

1 Make the filling: put the dried mushrooms in a bowl with the hot water and leave to soak for 2 hours.

2 Heat the butter and olive oil in a large frying pan over medium heat. Stir in the parsnips and cook for 8-12 minutes, until they are almost soft. Add the ginger and garlic and stir for 1 minute. Increase the heat and add the apricots and mushrooms with their soaking liquid. Allow

to bubble, without stirring, for about 2 minutes, until the liquid has been almost completely absorbed.

3 Transfer to a mixing bowl. Drain the chestnuts, chop roughly and stir into the parsnip mixture. Add the walnuts and mix gently with a wooden spoon. Season to taste with salt and pepper.

4 Make the crackers: melt the butter over low heat and use to brush the sheets of filo pastry and sandwich them together. Use 4 sheets of pastry for each cracker, brushing with butter between sheets. Divide the filling mixture between the 4 crackers, placing it along the centre of each rectangle and leaving some space at each end.

5 Roll up each cracker and tie each end with a little string to resemble a real cracker. Snip the ends with a pair of scissors to make them look realistic. Brush with melted butter and place them on an oiled baking tray. Bake in a preheated oven at 220°C/425°F/Gas Mark 7 for 20 minutes, until golden brown.

6 Remove the string and replace with fine ribbon. Serve with Cranberry Orange Sauce (see page 46).

SERVES: 4

Below: Filo Crackers

THE CHRISTMAS PUDDING

SUSAN BROOKES

HEATING AND SERVING THE CHRISTMAS PUDDING

To reheat and serve the Christmas Pudding (see the recipes on pages 16/17), steam it gently for 3 hours. Remove the foil and greaseproof paper and turn the pudding out on to a heatproof serving dish. You can decorate the pudding with a sprig of holly and serve it with Rum Sauce or Brandy Butter (see recipes below), or you can opt for a more flamboyant finish and serve it flaming with brandy.

The best way to light the brandy is to warm it in a metal ladle over a gas flame; otherwise, in a small saucepan over medium heat. Pour it quickly over the pudding and set alight with a match. Serve immediately while it is still flaming. Alternatively, your guests can add a little brandy themselves to their serving of Christmas Pudding.

RUM SAUCE

75g/3oz butter
75g/3oz plain flour
600ml/1 pint milk
75g/3oz caster sugar
4 tablespoons dark rum
150ml/5 fl oz single cream

1 Put the butter, flour and milk in a saucepan and whisk over medium heat. The sauce will thicken as it starts to simmer. Continue whisking but turn the heat down low. Cook for a further 5 minutes, stirring.
2 Add the sugar, stirring until dissolved, and then remove from the heat. Stir in the rum and then the cream. Cover the surface with cling film to prevent a skin forming and keep warm until required. Serve with Christmas Pudding.
SERVES: 8

BRANDY BUTTER

Boozy butters, such as this, are sometimes called hard sauces, which they are when cold. However, they melt deliciously when spooned over a hot pudding. They are the perfect accompaniment for Christmas Pudding, although you need only a little as they are so rich.

115g/4oz butter, softened
50g/2oz caster sugar
50g/2oz icing sugar
4 dessertspoons brandy

1 The butter has to be soft so take it out of the refrigerator in plenty of time. Place in a bowl with half of each of the sugars, and beat well together.
2 Add the brandy and the rest of the sugars and continue beating until the mixture goes white and soft. Cover with cling film and store in the refrigerator for up to 2-3 weeks.
SERVES: 10-12

Variation: To make Cumberland Rum Butter, make as above substituting rum for brandy, and soft brown sugar for caster sugar.

WINBY WAFERS

This is my producer's special family recipe for cheese biscuits. They are light and crisp - ideal with a well-matured Stilton.

225g/8oz plain flour
1/2 teaspoon salt
1 level teaspoon baking powder
50g/2oz butter or lard, diced
cold water, to mix
milk or beaten egg, to glaze
salt, sesame, caraway or poppy seeds, for sprinkling

1 Sieve the flour with the salt and baking powder into a mixing bowl. Rub in the butter or lard until thoroughly combined.

2 Add enough water to mix to a firm dough. Leave to stand for 10 minutes. Turn out on to a lightly floured surface and roll out very thinly.

3 Stamp into rounds with a glass tumbler and place the rounds on a lightly greased baking sheet. Brush with milk or beaten egg, and sprinkle with salt, sesame, caraway or poppy seeds.

4 Bake in a preheated oven at 200°C/400°F/Gas Mark 6 for 10-15 minutes, until crisp and golden. Cool on a wire rack and store in an airtight tin. Serve with cheese.

MAKES: approximately 20 biscuits

Below: Christmas Pudding

USING UP LEFTOVERS

TURKEY AND BARLEY SOUP

BRIAN TURNER

300ml/¹/₂ pint turkey stock
350g/12oz pearl barley
600ml/1 pint velouté sauce
225g/8oz turkey meat, diced
2 egg yolks
300ml/¹/₂ pint single cream
25g/1oz cooked macaroni
croûtons, to serve

1 Put the turkey stock in a large saucepan and simmer the pearl barley in the stock for 45 minutes, until cooked and tender.
2 Strain the stock into the velouté sauce and bring to the boil. Reduce the heat and add the diced turkey meat.
3 In a separate bowl, mix the egg yolks and the cream together. Pour a little of the soup into the egg and cream mixture, stir well and then pour back into the soup. Bring back to the boil, stirring all the time.
4 Remove from the heat and season to taste with salt and pepper. Stir in the macaroni and serve immediately with croûtons.
SERVES: 4

Tip: To make the velouté sauce, melt 50g/2oz butter and stir in the same quantity of flour. Add 900ml/1¹/₂ pints turkey stock and stir well until thick and smooth. Cook for 25 minutes.

TURKEY STOCK

Pick all the meat off the carcase and set aside. Chop the turkey bones and place in a large pan with a peeled onion, 2 carrots, some black peppercorns, a bay leaf, celery stick and 2-3 tomatoes. Bring to the boil, reduce the heat and simmer for 45 minutes. Cool and use for making soups and sauces.

STILTON, APPLE AND CELERY FILO ROLL

SUSAN BROOKES

1 garlic clove, crushed
300g/10oz leeks, washed, trimmed and sliced
225g/8oz celery, sliced
115g/4oz butter
1 red-skinned eating apple, cored and diced
225g/8oz blue Stilton cheese, cubed
6 spring onions, sliced
115g/4oz walnuts, chopped
2 tablespoons chopped fresh parsley
salt and pepper, to taste
5 large sheets filo pastry

1 Gently fry the garlic, leeks and celery in 25g/1oz of the butter for about 5 minutes, until the vegetables begin to soften. Transfer to a bowl and leave to cool.
2 Add the apple, Stilton and spring onions to the cooled leek mixture together with most of the walnuts (reserve a few for decoration). Mix well, adding parsley and seasoning to taste.
3 Heat the remaining butter over low heat. Spread out one sheet of filo pastry and brush with some of the melted butter. Lay another sheet of pastry on top and brush with more butter. Layer up the pastry sheets in this way, brushing each with melted butter, until they are all used up.
4 Place the filling along the centre of the pastry. Fold one long edge over the filling and then roll up like a Swiss roll, leaving the join underneath. Press the ends together to seal them. Brush with any remaining melted butter and sprinkle with the reserved walnuts.
5 Lift the roll carefully and transfer to a baking sheet. Bake in a preheated oven at 190°C/375°F/Gas Mark 5 for 30 minutes, until crisp and golden brown. Cut into thick slices to serve.
SERVES: 4-6

APPLE AND MINCEMEAT STRUDEL

SUSAN BROOKES

300g/10oz mincemeat
2 Bramley apples, peeled, cored and grated
1 tablespoon rum
4 sheets filo pastry
75g/3oz butter, melted
115g/4oz marzipan, chopped
50g/2oz icing sugar

1 Put the mincemeat and apples in a bowl and mix well. Stir in the rum and set aside while you assemble the pastry.
2 Place a sheet of filo pastry on a baking sheet and brush with some of the melted butter. Place a second sheet on top, brush with butter and continue building up the sheets in this way until they are all used, brushing generously with butter in between.
3 Spread the mincemeat mixture over the pastry, leaving a gap all the way round the edge, about 2.5cm/1 inch wide. Scatter the marzipan over the mincemeat, and then roll up the pastry carefully from the long side, rather like you roll up a Swiss roll.
4 Fold in the ends to seal the filling, and brush the pastry roll with any remaining melted butter. Mark the top diagonally with a sharp knife.
5 Bake in a preheated oven at 220°C/425°F/Gas Mark 7 for 30-35 minutes, until golden brown. Dredge thickly with icing sugar and serve warm, cut into slices, with cream or crème fraîche.
SERVES: 4-6

Below: Apple and Mincemeat Strudel

BOXING DAY FAMILY LUNCH

SUSAN BROOKES

MENU

GOLDEN GEESE

RUM-SOAKED APPLES

GOOSEBERRY SAUCE

ROAST POTATOES (SEE PAGE 106)

BROCCOLI OR GREEN BEANS

LEMON SYLLABUB

GOLDEN GEESE

Goose was always the traditional Christmas bird before the turkey was introduced from the New World. Of course, you can serve this recipe on Christmas Day if you prefer goose to turkey. Although it is a very rich meat, it need not be too fatty if you follow the instructions here and pour off the surplus fat.

2 × 4.5kg/10lb oven-ready geese
1 quantity Rum-soaked Apples or stuffing of your choice
salt and freshly ground black pepper

1 Stuff the geese with the Rum-soaked Apples or a stuffing of your choice. Place in the body cavity, stuffing from either end. Alternatively, you can just use some green leek tops and chopped apple.
2 Prick the skin of the geese all over and rub with a little salt and pepper. Cover the legs with spare fat taken from inside each goose. Wrap them in foil or baking parchment and place on a rack, breast-side up, in a large roasting pan. Put in a preheated oven at 200°C/400°F/Gas Mark 6.

3 For the cooking time, allow 20 minutes per 450g/1lb plus 30 minutes, about 3½ hours for each 4.5kg/10lb goose. After 1 hour, remove from the oven and turn each goose so that the back is upwards. Uncover to let it brown and baste with the surplus fat in the pan. Keep the legs covered. During the cooking time, keep checking that the skin is not burning; if it is getting too brown, cover with foil.
4 For the last 45 minutes of cooking, turn each goose over on to its back and uncover the breast to brown it. Baste with fat, and then pour off some of the surplus fat from the tin.
5 When cooked, remove the geese from the oven and lift on to a large carving dish. Cover with foil and leave to rest for about 20 minutes before carving.
SERVES: 12-14

Tip: You can cook the giblets for making gravy the day before roasting the goose. Cover the giblets with at least 2.5-3.5 litres/4-6 pints of water. Bring to the boil and simmer for 3-4 hours. Leave to cool and strain off the fat. To make the gravy, mix some flour with a little of the pan juices from the geese. Add some of the stock, and bring to the boil, stirring. Cook until thick and smooth.

RUM-SOAKED APPLES

675g/1½lb apples
12 tablespoons rum
10 sage leaves
2 eggs
450g/1lb fresh breadcrumbs
2 teaspoons ground mace

1 Peel, core and slice the apples. Put them in a bowl and pour the rum over the top. Turn the apples in the rum to coat them, and leave to soak for at least 3 hours.
2 Chop the sage leaves finely, and then beat the eggs. Add

to the apples with the breadcrumbs and mace, and stir well to mix thoroughly. Use to stuff the geese.
SERVES: 12-14

GOOSEBERRY SAUCE

You can use frozen gooseberries for this recipe if you cannot obtain fresh ones since they are rarely available at Christmas. Better still, make the sauce in the summer and freeze until Christmas to introduce the tart, fresh flavours of summer in the middle of winter!

450g/1lb gooseberries
150ml/¹/₄ pint water
50g/2oz butter, softened
75g/3oz sugar

1 Put the gooseberries and water in a saucepan and simmer gently over low heat until soft.
2 Push the gooseberries through a sieve, and then beat the butter and sugar into the warm fruit purée. Serve warm with roast goose.
SERVES: 12-14

LEMON SYLLABUB

900ml/1¹/₂ pints double cream
350g/12oz caster sugar
12 tablespoons dry sherry
juice of 3 lemons

For the decoration:
zest of 2 lemons
1 tablespoon water
2 tablespoons caster sugar

1 Put the double cream, sugar and sherry in a large bowl and whisk together until thick. Whisk in the lemon juice and spoon into 12-14 serving dishes or glasses. Chill in the refrigerator for at least 2 hours.

2 Make the decoration: cut the lemon zest into very thin strips. Put the water and sugar in a small saucepan and stir over low heat until the sugar dissolves. Bring to the boil, add the strips of lemon zest and continue boiling until thick and syrupy. Remove the lemon zest and use to decorate the syllabubs. Serve with tuiles biscuits (optional).
SERVES: 12-14

Below: Lemon Syllabub

BOXING DAY FAMILY DINNER

BRIAN TURNER

SEAFOOD CANNELLONI

225g/8oz potatoes, peeled and sliced
150ml/¹/₄ pint chicken or turkey stock
150ml/¹/₄ pint fish stock
2 garlic cloves, peeled
225g/8oz whiting or other white fish fillets
115g/4oz peeled, cooked prawns
4 tablespoons finely chopped parsley
salt and freshly ground black pepper
12 ready-made dried cannelloni tubes
150ml/¹/₄ pint cream
175g/6oz unsalted butter, diced

1 Bring the potatoes and stock to the boil. Add the garlic and boil until cooked. Add the fish and simmer until cooked.
2 Remove the potatoes, garlic and fish from the stock. Keep the stock for making the sauce. Put the potatoes, garlic and half of the fish in a food processor and process to a purée. Flake the reserved fish and mix into the purée with the prawns and 2 tablespoons of the parsley. Season

to taste with salt and pepper. Set aside to cool and set.
3 Blanch the cannelloni tubes in boiling water for 5 minutes. Remove and drain. Put the fish filling in a piping bag and pipe into each cannelloni tube. Leave to set. Steam the cannelloni for 3-4 minutes, until cooked.
4 Reduce the reserved stock by half and add the cream and butter, stirring until melted. Sieve and add the remaining parsley, and pour over the cannelloni.
SERVES: 4

HARICOT BEEF

16 pickling onions, skinned
900g/2lb stewing steak, cubed
2 tablespoons oil
25g/1oz flour
300ml/¹/₂ pint beef stock
1 bouquet garni (thyme, bay leaf and parsley)
pinch of salt
pinch of cayenne pepper
450g/1lb carrots, sliced
450g/1lb swede, cubed
1 tablespoon Worcestershire sauce
50g/2oz capers
2-3 tablespoons chopped parsley
25g/1oz chopped raw shallots
4 yolks of hard-boiled eggs, mashed

1 Boil the onions in a little water until cooked and tender. Drain and keep the cooking water.
2 Fry the steak in the oil, until browned. Add the flour and cook for 1-2 minutes. Add the stock, together with some of the onion cooking water.
3 Bring to the boil. Add the bouquet garni, salt and cayenne. Cover the pan and simmer gently for 1¹/₂ hours. Check the pan regularly and top up with more stock if necessary.

4 After 1½ hours, add the carrots, swede, the reserved onions and Worcestershire sauce. Cook for 30 minutes. Serve sprinkled with capers, parsley, shallots and egg yolks.
SERVES: 4-6

FIG AND DATE SYLLABUB

4 slices Christmas cake
2 teaspoons cognac
2 tablespoons icing sugar
115ml/4 fl oz double cream
25g/1oz caster sugar
50g/2oz chopped figs
50g/2oz chopped dates

1 tablespoon sherry
juice and grated zest of ½ orange
1 tablespoon chopped mixed nuts

1 Cut each slice of Christmas cake into a round shape and carefully scoop out a little of the centre. Place the cake circles on a baking sheet and sprinkle them with cognac and icing sugar. Place them in a preheated oven at 200°C/400°F/Gas Mark 6 until warm, about 5 minutes.
2 Whip the cream with the sugar until it holds its shape. Fold in the fruit, sherry, orange juice and zest.
3 Place the warmed cake circles on 4 serving plates and spoon the cream into the middle. Sprinkle with nuts.
SERVES: 4

Below: Seafood Cannelloni

BOXING DAY SPECIAL DINNER

BRIAN TURNER

SPINACH, BACON AND EGG SALAD

675g/1¹/₂lb uncooked young spinach leaves
4 hard-boiled eggs, peeled
4 rashers fried bacon, crumbled
croûtons, to serve

For the dressing:
3 tablespoons olive oil
1 tablespoon white wine vinegar
1 teaspoon Dijon mustard
salt and freshly ground black pepper

1 Wash and dry the spinach leaves thoroughly. Remove any hard stems, and place the leaves in a large salad bowl.
2 Separate the egg yolks and whites. Chop the whites into large cubes, and pass the yolks through a sieve.
3 Mix the dressing ingredients together until thoroughly combined. Toss the spinach in the dressing until all the leaves are coated. Sprinkle with the bacon and sieved boiled egg, and then top with croûtons.
SERVES: 4

FILET DE BOEUF EN CROUTE

450g/1lb fillet of beef
3 tablespoons oil
115g/4oz liver pâté
salt and freshly ground black pepper
splash of cognac
225g/8oz puff pastry
1 egg, beaten

For the mushroom duxelles:
1 shallot, finely chopped
25g/1oz butter
225g/8oz button mushrooms, finely chopped

For the herb pancakes:
50g/2oz plain flour
pinch of salt
1 egg
150ml/¹/₄ pint milk
2 tablespoons chopped herbs, e.g. parsley, tarragon, chives

1 Make the mushroom duxelles: sauté the shallot gently in the butter until softened but not browned. Add the mushrooms and cook over gentle heat until all the liquid has evaporated. Remove from the heat and set aside.
2 Make the herb pancakes: whisk the flour, salt and egg with a little milk until blended. Whisk in the remaining milk and herbs, and leave to stand for 20-30 minutes. Heat a little butter in a frying pan and pour in half of the batter mixture. Swirl it around the pan and cook until the underneath is golden brown. Flip the pancake over and cook the other side. Remove and keep warm. Make another pancake with the remaining mixture.
3 Trim the beef and then tie with string so that it retains a neat, cylindrical shape. Seal it all over, on the outside, in a frying pan of hot oil. Remove from the pan and discard the string.

4 Mix the mushroom duxelles mixture with the pâté. Season with salt and pepper and add a splash of cognac. Spread one side of the beef fillet with half the pâté mixture.
5 Roll out the puff pastry to a rectangle, 7.5cm/ 3 inches longer than the beef fillet, and 15cm/6 inches wider. Make diagonal cuts at each corner so that the meat can be wrapped in the pastry like an envelope.
6 Place the herb pancakes on top of the pastry, slightly overlapping each other. Put the fillet, pâté-side down on top of the pancakes. Smear the rest of the pâté over the top, and fold the pancakes over the beef fillet.
7 Brush the edges of the pastry with the beaten egg, and then fold over and seal well so that the fillet is completely enclosed. Turn the parcel over so that the seams are underneath, and place on a baking sheet. Brush with beaten egg and place in the refrigerator for several hours.
8 Bake in a preheated oven at 200°C/400°F/Gas Mark 6 for 10 minutes, and then lower the oven temperature to 160°C/325°F/Gas Mark 3 for a further 15 minutes.
SERVES: 4

APPLE AND MANGO TARTS

225g/8oz puff pastry
15g/¹/₂oz butter
75g/3oz caster sugar
1 ripe mango, peeled, stoned and chopped
2 dessert apples
icing sugar, for dusting

1 Roll out the pastry thinly, about 2mm/¹/₈ inch thick, on a lightly floured board. Cut out 4 round discs, 10cm/ 4 inches in diameter.
2 Melt the butter, and add 50g/2oz of caster sugar and the mango. Stir well and cook gently to the consistency of jam, skimming off as much liquid as possible. Cool and then place a spoonful on each puff pastry disc.
3 Peel and core the apples, and slice them thinly, being careful to keep the apple shape. Arrange the slices in concentric circles on top of the mango jam. Sprinkle with the remaining caster sugar.

4 Place on a baking sheet and cook in a preheated oven at 200°C/400°F/Gas Mark 6. After 5 minutes, reduce the oven temperature to 180°C/350°F/Gas Mark 4 for a further 15 minutes, until the apples are cooked. Serve dusted with icing sugar.
SERVES: 4

Below: Filet de Boeuf en Croûte

PART SIX

PARTY TIME

Christmas is a special time to entertain, and most people have a buffet, drinks party or special get-together dinner for family, friends and neighbours. In the following pages, Susan Brookes and Brian Turner have devised some mouthwatering spreads for these special occasions, with recipes for enticing party nibbles and dips, cold buffet dishes and a stylish New Year's Eve dinner party.

DRINKS PARTY

SUSAN BROOKES

The best job at a drinks party is handing round the canapés; that way, you don't get stuck in a corner. You have to circulate and move on, but slowly if the company is good. It is impressive to offer a few hot nibbles and a choice of dips, and it need not take up too much of your time as many can be made in advance. In addition to the recipes given here, you could also serve the following hot snacks: Savoury Muffins and Crispy Baked Skins (see page 96).

SPICED CHICKEN WINGS

24 chicken wings

For the marinade:
5 garlic cloves, crushed
2.5cm/1-inch piece of fresh root ginger, peeled
and crushed
juice of 2¹/₂ lemons
6 tablespoons soy sauce
6 tablespoons clear honey
1 teaspoon chilli flakes

1 Mix together all the marinade ingredients and pour into a lightly greased, large ovenproof dish. Add the chicken wings and turn them in the marinade until thoroughly coated. Cover the dish and leave for 2 hours in a cool place, or up to 24 hours in the refrigerator.
2 Bake the chicken wings in a preheated oven at 200°C/400°F/Gas Mark 6 for 20 minutes, until the chicken is coated with a sticky glaze and cooked through. Turn the chicken wings and baste them halfway through cooking.
SERVES: 8-12

GUACAMOLE

2 ripe avocados, skinned and stoned
¹/₂ onion
juice of ¹/₂ lemon
2 teaspoons tomato chutney
salt and freshly ground black pepper
2 teaspoons olive oil
¹/₂ teaspoon ground coriander
1 garlic clove, crushed
dash of Tabasco

1 Mash the avocado flesh. Press the onion over a lemon squeezer to extract a teaspoonful of juice.
2 Add the onion juice to the mashed avocado with all the remaining ingredients. Mix well together, and serve with tortilla chips or bite-sized raw vegetables (crudités).
MAKES: approximately 300ml/¹/₂ pint

THIS MORNING DIP

50ml/2 fl oz natural yogurt or fromage frais
175ml/6 fl oz soured cream
juice of 1 lime
salt and freshly ground black pepper
1 tablespoon snipped chives
1 tablespoon finely chopped parsley
1 tablespoon chopped oregano

1 Mix together the yogurt and soured cream, and then stir in the remaining ingredients.
2 Cover and chill thoroughly in the refrigerator. Serve as a dip with a selection of crudités, e.g. radishes, cauliflower and broccoli florets, strips of red, yellow and green pepper, button mushrooms, celery sticks etc.
MAKES: 225ml/8 fl oz

CHESTNUT CROQUETTES

1 stick celery
¹/₂ onion
25g/1oz butter
1 x 400g/14oz can chestnut purée
1 egg, beaten
salt and freshly ground black pepper
oil for deep-frying

For the coating:
25g/1oz seasoned flour
1 egg, beaten
dried breadcrumbs, for coating

1 Chop the celery and onion finely in a food processor with the metal blade fitted. Melt the butter in a saucepan and add the celery and onion. Cook gently for 5-10 minutes, until softened. Remove from the heat and transfer the cooked celery and onion to a bowl.

2 Mix in the chestnut purée with a fork, and add the beaten egg and seasoning to make a stiff paste that you can shape into small balls.

3 Roll each ball in seasoned flour, and then dip in beaten egg and coat with breadcrumbs. Deep-fry them in hot oil until crisp and golden. Drain on absorbent kitchen paper and serve hot. *(Photograph on preceding pages)*
MAKES: 20-24

Below: Spiced Chicken Wings, Guacamole and crudités

New Year's Eve Party - Cold Buffet

SUSAN BROOKES

MENU

BOMBED BEEF (SEE PAGE 32)

HONEY GLAZED HAM (SEE PAGE 32)

STILTON AND WALNUT PIE (SEE PAGE 34)

CONFITURE D'OIGNONS (SEE PAGE 38)

RED SALAD

GREEN RICE

WHITE CHOCOLATE CHEESECAKE

RED SALAD

2 large carrots
1 radicchio, washed and leaves separated
4 medium boiled beetroots (not pickled), cut into sticks
4 tomatoes, skinned and sliced
2 red peppers, seeded and cut into strips
bunch of radishes, trimmed and sliced
1 small punnet of strawberries, hulled and halved (optional)

For the dressing:
50g/2oz Red Windsor cheese, crumbled
2 tablespoons olive oil
1/2 tablespoon red wine vinegar
1 heaped teaspoon tomato purée
3 tablespoons orange juice
1 garlic clove, crushed
dash of Worcestershire sauce
salt and freshly ground black pepper

1 Make the dressing: combine all the ingredients, except the salt and pepper, by whisking or whizzing together in a blender or food processor. Season to taste. If wished, you can make this a day or two in advance and store in the refrigerator until needed.
2 Peel the carrots, cut into sticks and then blanch for 2 minutes in boiling salted water. Drain and refresh under running cold water, and drain again. Arrange with the other vegetables and strawberries on a large platter, and just before serving drizzle the dressing over the top.
SERVES: 8

GREEN RICE

3 tablespoons green pesto sauce
300g/10oz long-grain rice
600ml/1 pint vegetable stock
6 spring onions, thinly sliced
2 tablespoons olive oil
1 tablespoon lemon juice
salt and freshly ground black pepper

1 Mix 1 tablespoon of the pesto sauce with the uncooked rice, making sure that all the grains are coated. Set aside for at least 10 minutes.
2 Put the pesto-coated rice in a saucepan with the stock, and bring up to the boil. Reduce the heat and then simmer, partially covered, for about 20 minutes, until the rice is cooked and tender and has absorbed all the liquid. Keep checking the rice near the end of cooking time in order to prevent it boiling dry; you can add a little more stock or water, if necessary.
3 Tip the cooked rice into a large bowl and stir in the spring onions, olive oil, lemon juice and the remaining pesto sauce. Stir until well coated, season to taste with salt and pepper, and serve warm or cold.
SERVES: 6-8

WHITE CHOCOLATE CHEESECAKE

75g/3oz butter
300g/10oz half chocolate-coated wholewheat biscuits

For the filling:
2 x 150g/5oz packets good-quality white chocolate
50g/2oz butter, softened
50g/2oz caster sugar
450g/1lb cream cheese
3 eggs, beaten

For the topping:
150ml/¼ pint double cream, whipped
white chocolate flake or chocolate curls
cocoa powder for dusting

1 Make the base: melt the butter in a small saucepan. Grind or crush the biscuits into crumbs, and mix into the melted butter. Press the crumb mixture into the base of 1 large or 2 medium-sized greased and lined tins.

2 Make the filling: break the white chocolate into pieces and place in a bowl set over a pan of barely simmering water, until melted. Remove from the heat. Cream the butter, sugar and cream cheese together, and then stir in the melted chocolate. Mix well and stir in the beaten eggs.

3 Pour the mixture into the prepared tin(s), and bake for 35-45 minutes in a preheated oven at 170°C/325°F/Gas Mark 3, until just set and browned on top. Leave to cool in the tin(s).

4 Turn the cheesecake(s) out of the tin(s) and spread the cream over the top. Decorate with crumbled flake or chocolate curls, and dust with cocoa powder.

SERVES: 10-12

Below: White Chocolate Cheesecake

NEW YEAR'S EVE DINNER

BRIAN TURNER

MENU

GRAVADLAX

ROAST DUCK STUFFED WITH APPLES AND PRUNES

RED CABBAGE WITH CRANBERRIES (SEE PAGE 107)

CARAMELIZED POTATOES (SEE PAGE 107)

SWEDISH RICE PUDDING

GRAVADLAX

900g/2lb fresh salmon, boned and filleted
1 large bunch of fresh dill, chopped
50g/2oz coarse sea salt
50g/2oz caster sugar
freshly ground black pepper
sprigs of fresh dill, to garnish

For the mustard sauce:
3 egg yolks
115g/4oz German mustard
25g/1oz brown sugar
150ml/¹/₄ pint olive oil
splash of white wine vinegar
2-3 tablespoons finely chopped dill

1 Place one fillet of the fish, skin-side down, in a deep glass, enamel or stainless steel dish. Scatter the dill over the fish. In a separate bowl, combine the salt, sugar and black pepper, and sprinkle over the fish.

2 Cover with the remaining fillet of salmon, skin-side up, and then cover with aluminium foil. Place a heavy dish on top and weight it down with metal weights or cans.

3 Refrigerate for 24 hours, turning the fish every few hours and basting it with the marinade that forms in the dish. When ready to serve, remove the salmon from the marinade and scrape away the dill and seasonings. Pat dry.

4 Make the mustard sauce: whisk the egg yolks and mustard until well blended. Whisk in the sugar. Gradually whisk in the olive oil in a thin stream and then stir in the vinegar and dill.

5 Place the salmon, skin-side down, on a carving board and slice thinly on the diagonal. Serve, garnished with sprigs of dill, with the mustard sauce.
SERVES: 6-8

ROAST DUCK STUFFED WITH APPLES AND PRUNES

2 × 2.5kg/5lb duck
¹/₂ lemon
2 onions, chopped
2 apples, peeled, cored and chopped
24 prunes, soaked overnight, stoned and chopped

1 Rub inside the ducks with the cut lemon. Mix the chopped onions, apples and prunes and place inside the neck cavity of each duck. Sew up the entrance with thread.

2 Place in a roasting pan and cook in a preheated oven at 180°C/350°F/Gas Mark 4 for 1¹/₄ hours. After 30 minutes turn the ducks over. They are cooked when the juice runs clear when pierced with a skewer.

3 Leave the ducks to stand for 15 minutes. Before carving, remove the fruit stuffing and serve with the ducks.
SERVES: 6-8

SWEDISH RICE PUDDING

450ml/³/₄ pint milk
25g/1oz caster sugar
90g/3¹/₂oz long-grain white rice
75g/3oz blanched almonds, chopped
50ml/2 fl oz sherry
1 teaspoon vanilla essence
115ml/4 fl oz double cream, chilled
cherry liqueur, to serve (optional)

1 Put the milk in a heavy saucepan and bring to the boil. Stir in the sugar and rice, then lower the heat and simmer, uncovered, for about 25 minutes, until the rice is quite soft, but not mushy.

2 Pour the rice immediately into a shallow bowl to cool it quickly. Stir in the almonds, sherry and vanilla.

3 Whip the cream in a chilled bowl until it thickens and holds its shape softly. Fold it into the tepid rice mixture, and transfer to a serving dish. Chill in the refrigerator until ready to serve. If wished, you may serve this with a spoonful of cherry liqueur poured over the top.

SERVES: 6-8

Below: Gravadlax with Mustard Sauce

A NEW START

ROSEMARY CONLEY

HOW TO ENJOY CHRISTMAS
WITHOUT RUINING YOUR DIET

Each year as Christmas approaches, I have to admit to just a touch of apprehension. Even if I have managed to stay on top of controlling my weight for most of the year, there is always the danger of so much damage being done over Christmas and the New Year. At this special time, we want to treat our family to lots of goodies that we wouldn't usually buy; and we tend to stock up the store cupboard in the weeks leading up to Christmas. Then on Christmas Day we proudly display a magnificent selection of delicious delicacies, and we are often too full up to eat the chocolates, Turkish delight and nuts, which remain barely touched. When the festivities are over, because we can't bear to see food wasted, we eat them – and that is where the real damage is done.

I would never expect anyone to lose weight over Christmas, and I do think that we should allow ourselves lots of treats as it very important for the dieter to feel that he or she is not missing out. I have discovered that when I have been positively saintly over Christmas, my willpower has subsequently disintegrated around the New Year. However, I have now resolved this problem and I know that we actually *need* to overeat at Christmas. Having a bit of a blow-out and then feeling uncomfortable afterwards reminds us of how much better we feel when we do eat sensibly.

So by making a few simple changes to the way in which I prepare the festive food in order to minimize the damage, now I am able to spoil myself or even over-indulge, and I never feel that I am going without and missing out on all the traditional Christmas dishes. On this basis, I can eat as much as I want to on both Christmas Day and Boxing Day. The following day, I feel so over-full that I start my Christmas Binge Corrector Diet. Any excess weight swiftly disappears and I go back to eating sensibly from then onwards.

Here are some really low-fat, low-calorie recipes for Christmas lunch to help the damage limitation process even further.

ROAST TURKEY

1 × 5.4kg/12lb fresh turkey
Celery, Apricot and Chestnut Stuffing
600ml/1 pint chicken stock
2 tablespoons gravy powder (not granules)
2 chicken stock cubes or stock made from turkey giblets

1 Wash the turkey thoroughly in cold water and remove the giblets and any fat. Fill the neck end with the prepared stuffing mixture. Do not use any fat.

2 Pour the chicken stock into a large roasting pan and place the turkey on a wire rack above it in the pan. Cover with aluminium foil and place in a preheated oven at 180°C/350°F/Gas Mark 4, allowing a cooking time of 15 minutes per 450g/1lb plus 20 minutes over. Note that a larger bird weighing in excess of 6.3kg/14lb should be cooked for 12 minutes per 450g/1lb plus 20 minutes over.

3 Turn the roasting pan round every hour to ensure even cooking. One hour before serving, remove the turkey from the oven and remove the foil. Pour off most of the cooking liquid into a large bowl or jug. Return the turkey (without the foil) to the oven for 30 minutes.

4 Meanwhile, place 4 large ice cubes in the turkey liquid. After 5 minutes, place the liquid in the refrigerator or freezer in order to cool it as fast as possible. The fat will then separate and thicken, allowing it to be removed before making the gravy.

5 Mix the gravy powder with 150ml/¼ pint cold water and add the chicken stock cubes or some home-made turkey stock – made by boiling the turkey giblets in water for 45 minutes, cooling it and removing the fat. Keep the uncooked gravy to one side, awaiting the separated turkey liquid and any strained vegetable water from the cooked vegetables.

6 Thirty minutes before serving, remove the turkey from the oven and pierce one of the legs with a skewer or sharp knife. If the juice runs out clear, the bird is cooked; if it is coloured with blood, return the turkey to the oven for a little longer. Leave the cooked turkey to stand in a warm place for 30 minutes, covered with the reserved foil to keep it moist and warm. This 'resting time' will make carving easier.

7 Make the gravy: add the separated turkey liquid and strained vegetable water to the uncooked gravy mixture. Bring to the boil and then simmer gently until ready to serve. SERVES: 8-10

CELERY, APRICOT AND CHESTNUT STUFFING

1 head of celery
75g/3oz dried apricots, soaked overnight, or 115g/4oz no-soak apricots
150g/5oz chestnuts, fresh or canned
2 medium onions, chopped
1½ wine glasses white wine
115g/4oz fresh breadcrumbs
1 tablespoon chopped fresh parsley
salt and freshly ground black pepper

1 Prepare the ingredients by washing and trimming the celery and chopping it finely. Chop each apricot into 4 or 5 pieces. Blanch the fresh chestnuts (if using) in boiling water for 2 minutes, and then drain and peel off the skins while hot.

2 Dry-fry the onions in a non-stick frying pan until soft and brown. Add the wine, celery, apricots and chestnuts. Cook briskly over high heat for about 4 minutes, stirring continuously. Remove from the heat and then transfer the mixture to a large bowl. Allow to cool.

3 When cool, add the breadcrumbs, parsley, salt and pepper. Stir well, adding more breadcrumbs if necessary to make a firm mixture. Use to stuff the turkey.
SERVES: 8-10

DRY ROAST POTATOES

Choose medium potatoes of an even size. Peel and then put in a pan of cold salted water and bring to the boil. Drain and lightly scratch the surface of each potato with a fork. Sprinkle lightly with salt and place on a non-stick baking tray, without fat. Bake in a preheated oven at 200°C/400°F/Gas Mark 6 for 1-1½ hours.

LOW-CALORIE CHRISTMAS PUDDING

75g/3oz currants
75g/3oz sultanas
115g/4oz raisins
4 tablespoons brandy, rum or beer
75g/3oz glacé cherries, halved
75g/3oz plain or self-raising flour
1 teaspoon mixed spice
¹/₂ teaspoon cinnamon
50g/2oz fresh breadcrumbs
50g/2oz muscovado or caster sugar
2 teaspoons gravy browning
grated zest of ¹/₂ lemon
grated zest of ¹/₂ orange
115g/4oz grated apple
115g/4oz finely grated carrot
1 tablespoon lemon juice
2 eggs
4 tablespoons milk
2 tablespoons molasses or cane sugar syrup

For reheating:
4 tablespoons rum or brandy

1 Soak the dried fruit in the rum, brandy or beer, and leave overnight. When ready to make the pudding, shake the cherries gently in the flour and then add the spices, breadcrumbs, sugar and gravy browning.

2 Mix in the grated zest, apple and carrot, together with the lemon juice. Beat the eggs with the milk and molasses and slowly add to the mixture, stirring well. Mix together gently and thoroughly.

3 Place in a 1.2 litre/2-pint ovenproof basin. If you are going to microwave the pudding, place an upturned plate over the basin and microwave on HIGH for 5 minutes. If steaming the pudding, cover with foil or a pudding cloth, and then steam gently for 3 hours – this makes a moister pudding.

4 After cooking, allow the pudding to cool and then wrap in aluminium foil and leave in a cool, dry place until required. Before reheating, pierce the pudding several times with a fork and pour some more rum or brandy over the top. Steam for 1-2 hours. If wished the pudding can be frozen, but it must be thawed thoroughly before reheating.
SERVES: 8-10

BRUSSELS SPROUTS WITH CHESTNUTS

450g/1lb chestnuts
450-900g/1-2lb Brussels sprouts
375ml/13 fl oz chicken stock
freshly ground black pepper

1 Make a small nick in each chestnut with a sharp knife, and then blanch them quickly in boiling water for 2 minutes. Peel off the skins while hot.

2 Trim and wash the sprouts and cook in boiling salted water until just tender.

3 Meanwhile, place the chestnuts in a small saucepan with the stock. Cover and cook gently until the chestnuts are soft and the stock has been absorbed.

4 Gently mix the chestnuts with the sprouts in a serving dish and sprinkle with black pepper. Cover and keep warm until ready to serve.
Serves 6-10

STOP THE CHRISTMAS BINGE

1 Plan all the Christmas meals in advance, and buy only what you need; avoid impulse purchases.

2 Eat your Christmas feast at lunchtime so that you have time to work it off with a brisk walk.

3 Don't buy ready-shelled nuts; you'll eat far fewer having to crack each one.

4 Only open one box of Christmas chocolates at a time. Give any leftover unopened ones to a local old people's home or hospital.

CHRISTMAS BINGE CORRECTOR DIET

Christmas is undoubtedly the time when most people gain weight, and therefore I have named this regime the Christmas Binge Corrector Diet. However, it is also suitable for counteracting the results of any period of over-indulgence. Whatever the cause, it is essential that you go on this corrector diet immediately after your over-indulgence – leaving it for a week will not have the same effect. Also, you should not follow it for more than the recommended two days. If you do, you will bring your metabolic rate down and will regain your lost weight when you stop.

I believe that two days is the maximum period that we can go on a lower-calorie diet without adversely affecting our metabolism. If you follow this sharp, two-day plan, you will be amazed at how much of the weight you have gained over the Christmas period disappears.

DAY 1

DAILY ALLOWANCE

250ml/10 fl oz skimmed or semi-skimmed milk

BREAKFAST

1 whole fresh grapefruit
1 glass of sparkling mineral water

LUNCH

Large salad of lettuce, cucumber, tomatoes, grated carrot, grated cabbage, watercress with oil-free dressing **plus**
25g/1oz cooked chicken, ham **or** turkey **or** 50g/2oz cottage cheese
125g/5oz diet yogurt

DINNER

1 wedge of melon
100g/4oz white fish **or** 75g/3oz cooked chicken, served with unlimited vegetables, e.g. broccoli, cabbage, carrots, cauliflower, celery, spinach **plus**
2 tablespoons tomato sauce (for the fish) or 75ml/3 fl oz thin gravy (with the chicken)
1 piece of fresh fruit

DAY 2

DAILY ALLOWANCE

250ml/10 fl oz skimmed or semi-skimmed milk

BREAKFAST

1 Weetabix or 25g/1oz Allbran, 1 teaspoon sugar and milk from allowance
1 glass of sparkling mineral water

LUNCH

125ml/5 fl oz unsweetened fruit juice
1 slimmer's cup-a-soup **plus** 1 slice light wholemeal bread
125g/5oz diet yogurt **plus** 1 piece of fresh fruit

DINNER

1/2 grapefruit
75g/3oz cooked chicken **or** turkey (no skin), served with unlimited vegetables, e.g. broccoli, carrots, cabbage, celery, cauliflower **plus** a little thin gravy
1 piece of fresh fruit

THE NEW YEAR RESOLUTION

There's nothing like a brand New Year to make a commitment for a New You – to lose weight and get in shape for the year ahead. Once you have established those good habits, you are set up for the rest of the year.

You should aim for leanness, not thinness; and fitness, not fanaticism, when it comes to getting into shape. Losing those unwanted pounds and increasing your level of fitness isn't going to happen instantly, just as you didn't become overweight or unfit overnight. Sensible low-fat eating and regular enjoyable exercise are habits that need to be acquired over a period of time, and once they become part of your everyday life you will soon reap the benefits. Perhaps the greatest news of all is that it's never too late to start.

Once you have made the decision to make some changes and to stop inventing excuses for your lack of success in the past, you have to set some plans into action. Use up all the high-fat food that is lurking in the fridge, and re-educate the shopping trolley and the frying pan. This is fundamental if you are to embark on a healthy "eat well and feel brilliant" eating plan. The only way to win is to want to win badly enough. Here are some simple rules:

1 Eat three meals a day. Breakfast is essential to kick-start the metabolism, and a vital part of a successful weight loss campaign. Lunch should fit into your everyday life; even if you dine out every day you can still choose low-fat, low-calorie food from the menu. If it's not on the menu, ask!

Aim to satisfy your hunger but not to spoil your appetite for later. At dinner, fill up with lots of healthy vegetables and add some white meat or poultry cooked without any fat. Experiment with fruit and some of the low-calorie, low-fat ice creams.

2 Make a rule not to eat anything between meals. Snacking is probably the biggest single reason why many diets fail. Abstaining from all nibbles will ensure that you lose the maximum weight in the minimum time.

3 Stop spreading butter or margarine or low-fat spread on your bread. Instead, spread a low-calorie, low-fat dressing or, better still, nothing at all. Jam or marmalade tastes delicious spread straight on to bread or toast.

4 Remove temptation from your kitchen or workplace. Don't keep bars of chocolate or biscuits in your desk drawer – give them away now. Ask yourself: "Do I want the chocolate more than I want to be slim?"

5 Learn to cope with the difficult times. It's never easy to be good all the time when you are trying to lose weight. Don't throw in the towel after one indiscretion. When you have had one cheat, try to forget it – simply write it off – and just carry on with the diet.

6 A reducing diet should contain around 1400 calories a day for women, and 1700-1800 calories a day for men. Fat should be kept to a minimum. However, you should try to include some fatty fish within your eating plan as this food contains valuable nutrients.

If you wish to lose weight you must ask yourself how much you want to succeed. You will certainly need to make sacrifices and you will also have to make some difficult choices, but the rewards can be enormous. If you want to lose weight badly enough, you *can* do it – but the only person who can make that decision is you.

WHY EXERCISE?

The benefits of regular exercise are numerous. Not only does it help us to get fitter and healthier but it also relieves stress, burns fat and improves body shape. Just as food comes in lots of different forms and fulfills different roles, all of which are very important, so does exercise. We need a combination of different kinds of exercise to help us achieve optimum health and fitness. Here is a simple guide.

Aerobic exercise

This is any form of exercise that makes us out of breath, forcing more oxygen into the body. This sort of exercise makes the heart and lungs work harder and they become much stronger, which is vital to improving general health. Aerobic exercise is also a good fat burner. For maximum fat burning, work out at a moderate level (not to exhaustion) so that you are mildly perspiring and a little out of breath. At this level, the body calls on fat for additional fuel.

Good examples are: brisk walking, gentle jogging, swimming, aerobic or step classes, and dancing. Any amount is worth doing, and 20-30 minutes is a convenient time scale for most people. Try to do something every day. Warm up first by starting very gently and gradually building up the activity. Slow down at the end to cool off.

Toning exercises

These involve strength (pulling power) of the muscles and their endurance (staying power). You should repeat each exercise several times, ideally to a point of mild discomfort, and then do two more repetitions before resting the muscles you have been working. This can be done while you work another set of muscles. Return to the original exercise and repeat it. This enables the muscles to get bigger and stronger.

Stretching exercises

The greater our percentage of muscle compared to fat, the higher our metabolic rate. After "working" the muscles, we need to "stretch" them to help them relax and recover. Stretches should be held quite still for about 8-10 seconds and need to be performed just once. Stretches aid flexibility and help to reduce the risk of injury and muscle soreness.

Summary

Muscles require fuel to sustain them while fat requires none, so if you have more muscle and less fat your body will require more calories to maintain it which increases your metabolic rate. This is good news for the slimmer as it means you burn more calories just going about your everyday life. Try to incorporate a combination of aerobic and toning exercises within your

weekly programme of activities. Perseverance will pay dividends.

Remember that if you want to lose weight and get fitter, you need to change the bad eating habits that made you overweight in the first place, and you need to do more physical activity than you are used to. Start being more active. Take the stairs, not the lift. Park your car further away, do something physical in your lunch hour, even if it's only walking round the shops. The best sort of exercise is the exercise you actually do!

EXERCISE TIPS

● Exercise must be fun for you to continue.
● Work out to music as it will help to motivate you.
● Buy a fitness video and/or go along to a diet and fitness class to work out with other people and enjoy the camaraderie.
● Make exercise a regular part of your life and you'll live longer and look better for it.
● Exercise is one of the most effective tools in stress management. **Use it!**

THE WARM-UP

Always warm-up thoroughly before you exercise. It will prepare your body and stretch out tense muscles, helping you to avoid injury.

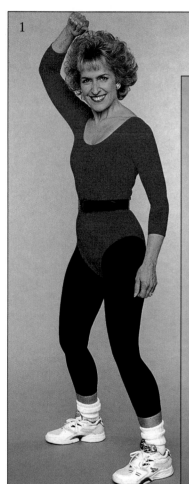

1 Rotate alternate arms backwards as if you are brushing your hair, transferring your weight from foot to foot. Repeat 16 times.

2 Step from side to side, tapping the opposite heel on the floor in front of you. Flex and straighten your arms as you step. Repeat 16 times.

3 Extend your legs to the side, alternately, tapping the floor with your heels and swinging your arms in and out. Repeat 16 times.

4 Raise alternate knees in front of you, pressing down with both arms. Be sure to keep your tummy tight and your back straight. Repeat 16 times.

5 Now kick back behind you with alternate feet, keeping your arms crossed in front of you. Repeat 16 times.

6 Rotate your hips in a clockwise direction 8 times. Then repeat 8 times in an anti-clockwise direction.

7 Extend alternate legs to the side, pointing your toes and swinging your arms from side to side. Repeat 32 times.

8 Keeping your hips square, twist your upper body only from side to side. Do it smoothly without jerking. Repeat 8 times to each side.

PREPARATORY STRETCHES

9 Back of Thigh Stretch Bend one knee and then, keeping your weight on that foot, extend the other leg in front with toes raised. Feel the stretch at the back of the knee and the thigh. Hold for 10 seconds, then change legs and repeat.

10 Calf Stretch Shift your weight on to the front leg and bend the knee. Your back leg is straight, heel on the floor, toes of both feet facing forwards. Feel the stretch in the calf muscle of your back leg. Hold for 10 seconds and repeat with the other leg.

11 Front Thigh Stretch Holding on to the back of a chair with your inside leg slightly bent, bend the other leg and take hold of your foot. Ease the foot back and up, with both knees aligned. Hold for 10 seconds. Release and repeat with the other leg.

AEROBICS

These exercises will make your heart and lungs work harder so that they become stronger and more efficient. If you do these exercises regularly, your general health, strength and stamina will all improve.

13 Bend your knees and pull an imaginary bow and arrow with your arms. Straighten the knees and repeat to the other side. Repeat 24 times on alternate sides.

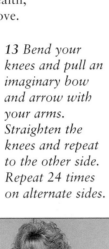

15 Tap the toes of one foot on the floor behind you, pushing your arms back as you step. Repeat 32 times with alternate feet.

12 Alternately bend and straighten your knees, pulling your elbows back at shoulder level and keeping your tummy pulled in tightly. Repeat 32 times.

14 Step and lunge to one side, reaching across with the opposite arm. Only the toes of the straight leg should touch the floor. Try to straighten the arm and leg as much as possible as you lunge. Repeat 24 times to alternate sides.

AEROBICS *Continued*

17 *Step to one side and curtsey, swinging your arms out and in to cross high above your head. Repeat 24 times.*

18 *Jog on the spot, flexing and bending alternate arms. Make sure your knees are soft and your heels are down when you land. Repeat 32 times.*

16 Extend alternate legs to the side, tapping the floor with your heels and swinging your arms in and out. Repeat 16 times.

TONING

19 *Inner Thigh Toner* *Place the foot of the top leg flat on the floor behind the lower leg. Raise the lower leg as high as possible. Your hips should remain square. Lower the leg and repeat 12-14 times. Roll over and repeat with the other leg.*

20 *Outer Thigh Toner* *Lie on your side with both knees bent. Raise and lower the top leg, keeping it bent. Make sure the hips are square and the knees and toes face forwards. Repeat 12-14 times, then roll over and repeat with the other leg.*

21 Upper Arm Toner Sit, with knees bent, propped up on your hands which should be at least 30cm/12 inches behind your back, fingers pointing forwards. Bend your arms so that your elbows move backwards, then straighten them again. Repeat 12-14 times.

22 Tummy Trimmer Lie on your back with knees bent and raised, tummy pulled in tightly. Pull the knees in towards your chest, pressing down with your tummy muscles to lift your hips slightly off the floor. Don't use your arms. Repeat 12-14 times.

23 Chest Toner Lie as shown (a), elbows bent and level with shoulders. Lift your arms and press the elbows together (b). Lower the arms and repeat 12-14 times.

24 Tummy Toner With feet on a chair, support your head with your hands. Pulling in the tummy, raise head and shoulders off floor. Your chin should not touch your chest. Raise on a count of 2, and lower on a count of 2. Repeat 12-14 times.

25 Bottom Toner Stand facing a chair and raise one leg behind you, keeping it straight and squeezing your seat as you raise. Lower the leg and repeat 12-14 times. Repeat with the other leg. Make sure you keep your tummy tight, hips square and back straight.

26 Waist Toner Lie down with knees bent. Supporting yourself with one arm, reach across your body with the other arm, pressing your tummy down. Take care not to roll the hips. Return to the floor and repeat 12-14 times each side.

COOL-DOWN STRETCHES

Always do a few simple cool-down stretches at the end of your work-out. They will ease out your muscles, especially if they are tired, and help to relax you.

27 Outer Thigh Stretch Lie down with your arms outstretched, both knees bent. Lower both knees slowly to one side, both feet on the floor. Hold for 10 seconds. Slowly raise knees to centre and repeat to other side.

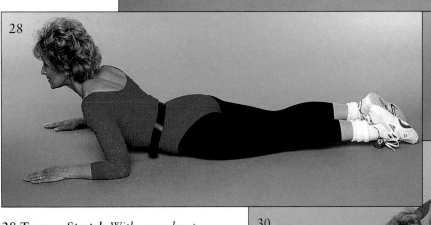

29 Inner Thigh Stretch Sit with knees bent, soles of feet together. Using your elbows, gently ease your knees down as far as is comfortable. Hold for 15 seconds.

28 Tummy Stretch With arms bent, slowly raise head and shoulders off the floor. Support yourself on your forearms and elbows. Feel the stretch down the front of your abdomen. Hold for 10 seconds.

30 Seat Stretch On all-fours, slowly ease your hips backwards without touching heels while extending your arms in front. Hold for 10 seconds.

32 Back of Upper Arm Stretch *Stand with feet apart and knees slightly bent. Raise one elbow and ease hand down your back, using other arm to assist. Hold for 10 seconds. Relax and repeat with the other arm.*

33 Chest Stretch *Take your arms behind you, placing one hand on top of the other. Raise your arms and feel the stretch across your chest. Hold for 10 seconds.*

31 Waist Stretch *With feet apart and knees slightly bent, one hand on thigh for support, lean to one side and reach the opposite arm over. Hold for 10 seconds and repeat to other side.*

34 Back of Thigh Stretch *Sit with one leg straight, the other slightly bent. Ease your chest forwards towards the straight leg and feel the stretch at the back of the knee and thigh. Hold for 10 seconds and then repeat with the other leg.*

STOCKISTS

Food

Susan Brookes

If you're looking for something a bit different from the usual chain store offerings, you can order some of the goodies that are available by post. There may also be local specialist suppliers in your area who run a gifts by post service. Here are some ideas for you to try; I have visited them all at various times and can vouch for them personally.

Abergavenny Fine Foods
Unit 4
Castle Meadows Park
Abergavenny
Gwent NP7 7RZ
Tel: 01873 850001
● Especially worthwhile for its range of Welsh cheeses, available as a selection of miniatures.

Betty's by Post
1 Parliament Street
Harrogate
North Yorkshire HG1 2QU
Tel: 01423 531211
● Particularly good for baked goods, many with a continental flavour. They also do excellent chocolates, specialist teas and coffees.

Chatsworth Farm Shop
Stud Farm
Pilsley
Bakewell
Derbyshire DE45 1UF
Tel: 01246 583392

● A range of beautifully packaged goods, and some fresh foods can be sent overnight.

Inverawe Smokehouses
Taynuilt
Argyll PA35 1HU
Tel: 01866 2446
● For smoked salmon traditionally smoked over oak chips, also other fish and gravadlax as well as smoked meats.

The Real Meat Company
East Hill Farm
Heytesbury
Warminster
Wiltshire BA12 0HR
Tel: 01985 840436
● A full range of meat and meat products from livestock reared without growth promoters and according to a special high-welfare code. Pork, lamb, beef, bacon, chicken and cheese supplied in various sizes.

The Scottish Gourmet
Thistle Mill
Station Road
Biggar
Scotland ML12 6LP
Tel: 01899 211001
● This food service operates like a book club. A small membership fee gives you the chance to order from a monthly selection of Scottish dishes.

The Village Bakery
Melmerby

Penrith
Cumbria CA10 1HE
Tel: 01768 81515
● All sorts of organic bakery produce, using free-range eggs and no additives. Puddings and cakes produced from the ancient wood-fired brick oven are especially good.

Richard Woodall
Lane End
Waberthwaite
Millom
Cumbria LA19 5YJ
Tel: 01657 7237
● For wonderful hams and bacon as it used to taste.

Wines

Charles Metcalfe

For cross-Channel shoppers, here is a selection of good wine stockists on the other side of the Channel.

Boulogne: The Grape Shop
Hoverspeed Port & 85-87 rue Victor Hugo
Calais: Bar à Vins
52 place d'Armes
Cherbourg: La Maison du Vin
71 Avenue Carnot
Dieppe: LC Vins
1 Grande-Rue
Dunquerque: Tastevins de Flandres
2 rue Dampierre
Le Havre: Chais de la Transat
Avenue Lucien Corbeaux
Roscoff: Les Caves de Roscoff
Ateliers 7, 8 & 9,
Zone de Bloscon

St Malo: Le Tastevin
9 rue Val
You can also order your cross-Channel purchases in advance from the following:

The Grape Shop (order on 0171 924 3638, collect in Boulogne)
La Maison du Vin (order on 01929 480352, collect in Cherbourg)
Wine Collectors Club (order on 01306 881062, collect in Boulogne)
The Wine Society (order on 01438 740222, collect from Hesdin, an hour from Calais)

Wine by mail order

Adnams
The Crown
High Street
Southwold
Suffolk IP18 6DP
Tel: 01502 724222
● Wine side of excellent Suffolk brewer, one of the best lists in Britain.

Australian Wine Club
Tel: 01800 716893
● Mail order only specialist in Australian wines. Terrific selection.

The Beer Cellar
Forge Court
Reading Road
Yateley
Surrey GU17 7RX
Tel: 01252 861875
● The UK's best mail-order

beer supplier, with beers from Germany to the Ukraine.

Bibendum
113 Regent's Park Road
London NW1 8UR
Tel: 0171 722 5577
● Outstanding London-based merchant, very good on Burgundy, Rhone, Champagne and Italian wines.

Fine Wines of New Zealand
PO Box 476
London NW5 2NZ
Tel: 0171 482 0093
● The postcode tells the story: New Zealand wines, sold by a Kiwi, by mail order only. And they're good.

Gauntleys of Nottingham
4 High Street
Exchange Arcade
Nottingham NG1 2ET
Tel: 01602 417973
● Rhone, Alsace, Burgundy and port are among the strengths of this merchant.

Halves
Wood Yard, off Corve Street
Ludlow
Shropshire SY8 2PX
Tel: 01584 877866
● The best range of half-bottles in Britain, many bottled especially for this merchant.

Justerini & Brooks
61 St James's Street
London SW1A 1LZ
Tel: 071 493 8721

● Prices from this fabulous list are not as steep as you would imagine from the location in the heart of upper-class London.

Lay & Wheeler
6 Culver Street West
Colchester
Essex CO1 1JA
Tel: 01206 764446
● Wonderful selection of classic European and adventurous New World wines from Essex family company.

Laymont & Shaw
The Old Chapel
Millpool
Truro
Cornwall TR1 1EX
Tel: 01872 70545
● The best Spanish wine list in the country.

Tanners
26 Wyle Cop
Shrewsbury
Shropshire SY1 1XD
Tel: 01743 232400
● Family-run merchant with exemplary range of wines from everywhere.

Winecellars
153-155 Wandsworth High Street
London SW18 4JB
Tel: 0181 371 3979
● The best Italian wine list in Britain, but also strong on Australia and southern France.

The Wine Society
Gunnels Wood Road
Stevenage
Hertfordshire SG1 2BG
Tel: 01438 741177
● There is a small fee for life membership, but that gets you free delivery anywhere in the UK of a great list of wines, young and old, stored in ideal conditions.

Yapp Bros
The Old Brewery
Mere
Wiltshire BA12 6DY
Tel: 01747 860423
● Ex-dentist specialist in wines from the Rhone, Loire and Provence.

Creative crafts stockists

Maggie Colvin

Angelic
Tel: 0171 284 3975
● For flower-shaped candles.

Celia Birtwell
Tel: 0171 221 0877
● For a wide range of beautiful fabrics.

Cherry Coleman Designs
Tel: 0181 675 9847
● A range of lovely decorative bows available by mail order.

Decorative Arts
Tel: 0171 371 4303
● For MDF wastepaper baskets and box kits and paints.

DIY Crackers
Tel: 01702 338053
● For bunches of snappers for making crackers.

Handover
Tel: 0171 359 4696
● Dutch metal and Wondersize by mail order.

Jerry's Home Stores
Tel: 0171 225 2246
● For festive plates and crockery.

Chris Kingdom
Long Acre
57 Kilne Ride
Wokingham
Berks
● For bow makers by mail order.

Liberon Waxes
Tel: 01797 367555
● For a superb range of gilding creams.

Paperchase
Tel: 0171 580 8496
● For conical wire shapes for making alternative Christmas trees and a range of coloured paper products.

Prices Candles
Tel: 0171 228 3345
● A complete range of assorted coloured candles.

Ribbon Renaissance
Tel: 01734 732888
● Supplier of bow makers, ribbons etc.

RECIPE INDEX